West Village Originals

West Village Originals

An Oral History of New York City's Most Unique Neighborhood

by
Michael D. Minichiello

βιος Books
New York, NY

All interviews in this book previously appeared in *WestView News: The Voice of the West Village* from 2008–2020.

Cover and interior design: MDM Graphic Design, Inc.

βίος Books
An imprint of Woodwrit, Inc. Editions

WEST VILLAGE ORIGINALS. Copyright © 2021 by Michael D. Minichiello. All rights reserved, including the right to reproduce this book or portions thereof in any form whatsoever, allowing only for brief quotations in printed reviews. For information address Woodwrit, Inc. Editions, 135 West 10th Street, #11, New York, NY 10014.

ISBN: 978-1-949596-12-0

*For Bill
The best spouse, partner,
and editor*

I regret profoundly that I was not an American and not born in Greenwich Village. This is where it's happening.
—John Lennon

CONTENTS

INTRODUCTION 1
THE WEST VILLAGE 4
AUTHOR'S NOTE 7
THE INTERVIEWS:

ARCHITECTURE
    Barry Benepe 10
    James Stewart Polshek 12

BUSINESS
    Danny Bensusan 14
    Lisa Cannistraci 16
    Bill O'Donnell 18
    Nicky Perry 20
    Stephanie Phelan 22
    Billy Romp 24
    David Maurice Sharp 26
    Three Lives & Company 28
    Arnold S. Warwick 30

COMMUNITY ACTIVISM
    Keen Berger 34
    Andrew Berman 36
    Frederic Block 38
    Carmen Grange 40
    David Gruber 42
    Ralph Lee 44
    Joan McAllister 46
    Keith Michael 48
    Ethel Paley 50
    Allen Pilikian 52
    David Rothenberg 54
    Arthur Z. Schwartz 56
    Whitney North Seymour, Jr. 58

CULINARY ARTS
    Suzy Chase 62
    Anita Lo 64

DANCE
- Vincent Livelli 66
- Edith Stephen 68
- Vija Vetra 70

FILM & TELEVISION
- Page Johnson 74
- Karen Kramer 76
- Joe Lisi 78
- Victor Mignatti 80
- Sybil Sage 82
- Richard Eric Weigle 84

JOURNALISM
- James Lincoln Collier 86
- Mimi Sheraton 88
- Calvin Trillin 90
- Nancy Weber 92

MUSIC
- David Amram 96
- Bill Curreri 98
- David Del Tredici 100
- Bill Dunham 102
- Bobb Goldsteinn 104
- Larry Ham 106
- Peter Leitch 108
- Denise Marsa 110

PHOTOGRAPHY
- Maggie Berkvist 114
- Bob Gruen 116
- Rose Hartman 118
- David Plakke 120
- Suzanne Poli 122
- Nancy Rudolph 124
- Jan Staller 126
- SuZen 128

POETRY
- Edward Field 130
- George Held 132

THEATRE
- Charles Busch 136
- Peter Carlaftes 138
- Rainie Cole 140
- Barbara Garson 142
- David Greenspan 144
- Robert Heide 146
- Gordon Hughes 148
- Penny Jones 150
- Erwin Lerner 152
- Marshall W. Mason 154
- Scott Morfee 156
- Dina Paisner 158
- Everett Quinton 160
- William Repicci 162
- Salvador Peter Tomas 164
- David Van Asselt 166

VISUAL ARTS
- Isabel Case Borgatta 170
- Marjorie Colt 172
- Elliott Gilbert 174
- Stephen Hall 176
- Peter Harvey 178
- Rick Meyerowitz 180
- Kika Schoenfeld 182
- Jenny Tango 184
- Mary Vaccaro 186

WRITING
- Nancy Bogen 190
- Susan Brownmiller 192
- Jack Dowling 194
- John Gilman 196
- Catherine Revland 198
- Barbara Riddle 200
- Andrew Rubenfeld 202
- John Tytell 204

ACKNOWLEDGMENTS 206

INDEX 207

Jackson Square Park

Introduction

Photo: David Plakke

In 2008 I began to write for the West Village paper *WestView News*. I'm a graphic designer by profession and I called George Capsis, the publisher, in response to an ad he placed in his paper looking for someone to perform that function. However, when George found out that I had an MFA in film, he suggested I review movies for the paper instead. So, I did. But I soon discovered I enjoyed writing about other subjects even more, and before long I had the idea for a column called "West Village Originals." It occurred to me that there had to be many longtime West Village residents with interesting things to say about their lives, their careers, and the vast changes that have taken place in the area.

It turns out they did. They shared insights into times now past, amusing anecdotes of people and places that no longer exist, and poignant tales of what makes the Village such an inspiration to this day. They certainly reflected on the changes that have occurred through the years, but even this wasn't necessarily with regret. Instead, there was an overwhelming theme that spending so many years—oftentimes 40, 50, and 60—in the West Village had given them a quality of life they felt certain they never would have found anywhere else. This neighborhood has variously welcomed them, nurtured them, inspired them and, ultimately, made diehard fans of them all.

The funny thing is that I've never actually met most of the people I've profiled in person; all my interviews were done over the telephone. Interestingly, this created an atmosphere where my focus was on every word, without the distractions of in-person conversations. When each call ended, I felt I had truly taken an intimate journey through someone's life. Among the list of questions I would ask my favorite turned out to be, "Tell me about your parents." Invariably, this elicited touching and revealing responses, confirming that what their parents did for a living or enjoyed as hobbies had profound influences on their child's choice of a career.

At the end of each interview I had up to three pages of single-spaced copy that needed to be honed into an 800-word article. The challenge was to find the "hook" that introduced a defining theme and to present each person to be as interesting as they are; in other words, to do them justice. My greatest satisfaction was when those I interviewed expressed their sincere pleasure in being presented just as they might have hoped.

Over the years, I was privileged to interview so many icons and long-term residents who made the West Village their home. I was delighted that people like Calvin Trillin, Susan Brownmiller, or Joel Meyerowitz would so affably agree to talk to—and trust—someone who wrote for a local paper. I suppose that's what makes the West Village the special place it is, a sense of community that connects us regardless of one's position and celebrity. But as the neighborhood continues to change with the times, it seemed appropriate to capture in one collection the era in which my interviews were written.

These days I qualify as a West Village Original myself. Born in Nyack, New York to parents in the arts, I moved into the neighborhood in October 1974 while still a teenager. I always knew that one day I would live here. As with so many people I interviewed, my parents played a key role in that. When we were children they regularly introduced us to the joys of New York, and later as teenagers, my twin brother John and I spent many a day and night here. I was probably the last generation that could move into the West Village—albeit in a studio on Perry Street—and still manage it on my own. I always had a job and happily worked my way through college, first getting a BA from Hunter College and then an MFA from Columbia University's School of the Arts.

I know people like to talk of the horrible, crime-ridden days of the 70s and 80s in New York, but I had a wonderful time. There's nothing like being young for bravely plowing through the difficulties of life or finding what's exciting about your surroundings. There was a lot happening in the West Village. I loved Reno Sweeney on West 13th Street for its sophistication, Boots & Saddle on Christopher Street for its eclectic clientele, the Five Oaks on Grove Street where the great Marie Blake pounded the keys every night, and the Actors

Playhouse on Seventh Avenue South where I co-produced my first Off-Broadway play. But I'm glad that the City became so livable as I got older and settled down. And so full of trees! That I've also spent the last thirty-one years with my spouse, Bill, on Horatio Street has only added to the charm. I'm still loving my work as a graphic designer and have my own business now. We've been through a wonderful period of both relative peace and prosperity in New York. This makes me worry about the future as we emerge from the pandemic. Where we end up as a city and as neighbors is anybody's guess, but I'm counting on our inherent resilience to pull us through.

What is the biggest change for me when it comes to the West Village? It was always a desirable part of town, but the amount of money here now is staggering! My hope is that the next generation of residents will develop the same sense of allegiance to the neighborhood that defines those West Village Originals who came before them. They were—and continue to be—very special people and I'm happy to be among them. You all have my sincerest thanks for trusting me to tell your stories. They are now forever recorded as part of the history of our beloved West Village.

Michael D. Minichiello
New York City
Fall 2021

Little Island in the Hudson River

The West Village

The West Village is a neighborhood within the larger neighborhood of Greenwich Village, which was designated as a New York City historic district in 1969 and expanded since then. Situated on the island of Manhattan, it is bounded by the Hudson River on the west and Sixth Avenue on the east, extending from 14th Street south to Houston Street. Bordering neighborhoods include Chelsea to the north, the South Village and Hudson Square to the south, and Greenwich Village proper to the east. The neighborhood is primarily residential, with many small shops, restaurants, and services.

Notable features of the West Village include the Whitney Museum; Westbeth Artists Housing, one of the first examples of adaptive reuse of industrial buildings (in this case, Bell Laboratories) for artists and residents in the United States; the High Line, the elevated train tracks that once served businesses in the area, long abandoned and converted into a very popular public park; and other beautiful parks including Abingdon Square, Jackson Square, St. Vincent's, the AIDS Memorial, Hudson River Park along the water, and the newly opened, fanciful Little Island.

The Meatpacking District—also known as the Gansevoort Historic District—is at the north end of the West Village. Markets have existed in the district since the 1840s, and a number of meat-packing companies still operate here. Beginning in the 1990s, bars, restaurants, and boutiques have become far more common.

However, the appeal of the West Village extends well beyond its physical attributes of narrow cobblestone streets, abundant greenery, and low-rise, early-nineteenth-century architecture. Since 1916, when it first became known as "Little Bohemia," the West Village has nurtured generations of artists and activists who found refuge here from the greater metropolis of Manhattan. Names of past residents that quickly come to mind are Edna St. Vincent Millay and James Baldwin, Diane Arbus and Edward Albee. However, these are just the few of those who cemented the character of this neighborhood. In the pages of this book, you will read ninety interviews of those who still reflect the heartbeat of this unique community known as the West Village.

17 Grove Street

Abingdon Square Park

Author's Note

I began these interviews in 2008 when the West Village was going through enormous changes. During the following twelve years, that evolution only accelerated. A number of those featured in this book have since passed away. Many others have embarked on different journeys or fulfilled projects that were only dreams when they first shared their lives with me. However, the articles were not updated for this book and appear as they were originally published—timely snapshots of both those interviewed and of the West Village itself.

> *It's an amazing neighborhood. People are so supportive of not just their little independent bookshop, but all of the other shops as well. There's a very strong sense here about what makes their neighborhood special and a real community.*
>
> —Toby Cox,
> Three Lives & Company

Three Lives & Company Bookstore

West Village Original • Architecture

Barry Benepe
October 2012

Barry Benepe was born in Manhattan in 1928. After acquiring a degree in architecture from MIT, Barry became an urban planner and in 1976 started the Greenmarket revolution in New York City. He ran the organization for 22 years, retiring in 1998 to write and to continue to be active in his community as a volunteer.

"Two things I've always hated were the suburbs and the automobile," Barry Benepe confesses. As an architect, preservationist, and urban planner, he long felt that both had created the "homogenization" of the countryside and had blurred the distinction between country and city. "I've always wanted to keep that distinction alive," he says.

An opportunity to do just that arose in the mid-1970s when Benepe—after a foray into historic preservation—was doing planning work in New York City. One day he and his colleague, Bob Lewis, started talking about farmland loss and ways to halt it. "We were given $800 to raise foundation money to start farmer's markets to save farmland," he recalls. "At that time the food in New York was horrible so we dreamed up the idea of green markets. The foundations didn't think the city had the money to run the markets and so we decided to run them ourselves."

Was there a model for Greenmarket? "Yes. And this is where history comes in," Benepe answers. "Our city centers grew during a time when farms kept them alive with locally grown food. I was returning to a historic model that had been outdated for 100 years but was equally applicable today. To make it work I had to pragmatically develop the model to work in the field. It wasn't all that difficult because the farmers were doing so badly and they were very receptive to the idea."

In 1976, the first Greenmarket opened with 12 farmers in a parking lot on 59th Street and Second Avenue. A few months later Benepe and his team got a call from the head of the Manhattan Planning Department. "They were desperately trying to revive Union Square, which was going downhill very fast," he says. "Klein's Department Store was closing, there were drug dealers in the park, and things looked grim. They asked us to start a green market there but we were not very happy about doing it. However, the City really came on board and gave us all the necessary permits and the next mayor, Ed Koch, was a big supporter." Today, the Union Square Greenmarket is the jewel in the crown of a network that encompasses 54 markets. "And Greenmarket is self-supporting," Benepe adds. "It does not require foundation money because we're able to fund it through farmers' fees."

What was his greatest satisfaction through all of this? "Accomplishing the goals!" he readily admits. "Giving farmers a better living and getting better food on our tables. What's magical about Greenmarket is the enormous variety it offers consumers. It also brings in ingenuity and youth. The farmers—who are the real heroes in this story—first came in 1976 and now their children and grandchildren are coming to the markets. It's kept families farming. It's also satisfying because it's a team effort. I've gotten such wonderful heartfelt sentiments from the farmers."

Benepe has had his apartment on Jane Street since 1971 and shares it with his wife, Judith. True to his love of historic preservation, it's the neighborhood's sense of an earlier time that resonates with him. "It's the scale of the Village that I love," he says. "That and the fact that I live in a 19th Century environment. The streets are narrow and crooked. It's very special in that sense. We still have houses with gardens, and as Jane Jacobs would say, those who live on the ground floors have their 'eyes on the street.' We do shopping in very local stores and we even try to buy our clothing locally. It's like living in a true village and we love it."

"What's wonderful is that the Village isn't much different than it used to be," Benepe continues. Then he pauses for a moment. "If it is different, it's that the new people aren't as involved in volunteer community work as much as my peers used to be. Most of the things I accomplished in life I did as a volunteer, not as a paid professional. I did it because I wanted to control my environment. I just didn't want to be a passenger in life. I wanted to be a driver." He laughs. "I still do!"

West Village Original • Architecture

James Stewart Polshek

February 2015

Architect James Stewart Polshek was born in Akron, Ohio in 1930. He designed the Clinton Presidential Library in Arkansas and Santa Fe Opera and, closer to home, the Rose Center for Space at the Museum of Natural History, Scandinavia House, the Lycée Français, and the new entryway to the Brooklyn Museum. "Build, Memory," his look at a life in architecture, was published by The Monacelli Press recently.

Architect James Stewart Polshek speaks fondly of growing up in Akron, Ohio. "My parents got along very well," he says. "My mother was extremely orderly and she kept the house and our social life going. My father had this wonderful sense of humor and was beloved by everybody. He was very interested in politics and very sympathetic to Russia like a lot of progressive people at that time. I inherited a bit of both of them." It would be his mother's passion for order and his father's fervor for social issues that would come to define his career.

Polshek had actually begun studying medicine when one day he saw a modern house going up in his neighborhood. "It was very radical and I thought that was wonderful," he says. "As it began to go up I followed its progress, both inside and out. I soon started to build model houses at home. I stopped hanging around with my friends, let up on athletics even, and just built model houses. Eventually, I dropped pre-med and entered architecture school. One year later I transferred to Yale and got a graduate degree there." What did his parents think of this decision? "They were puzzled at first and may have even been a little disappointed," he says. "But not for long." After apprenticeships with I.M. Pei and Ulrich Franzen and a Fulbright Scholarship to Denmark, Polshek received his first major project designing a research lab in

Japan. He then returned to the United States, setting up his own firm in 1963.

If Polshek has a personal philosophy about architecture, it is his interest in buildings that serve the common good. "I feel that architecture has to have a broader definition," he says. "This was reinforced by some of the teachers that I had and by my experience in Pei's office. Very early on in my career I took on projects that encompassed historic preservation, non-profits, healthcare, and education; things that not every architect would jump at. Furthermore, I've always been more interested in doing additions to existing buildings. Both the Rose Center and the Brooklyn Museum are additions. I love adding something new to something old."

While some architects would argue otherwise, Polshek also believes that architecture is not an art form and—to a large extent—buildings make themselves. "An architect is both constrained and encouraged by costs, building codes, the site, climate, the rules of the municipality, and the specific needs of the client," he explains. "The actual ingredients are already there in the soup, but the architect puts in the seasoning. The style grows out of all those ingredients. This approach has always served me very well." Then he laughs. "This isn't something architects ordinarily give away, though!"

Polshek and his wife, Ellyn, moved to the Village in the early 60s and, since 1973, have lived on Washington Square. "It was very different back then," he says. "It was grungier but more hospitable to experimentation. In addition, the wealth that seeps out of every manhole cover and keyhole today was really absent. In 1973 our building was full of relatively young people with kids. Now apartments sell here for $3 or $4 million! It was that affordability that's probably the single biggest difference from now." At the end of the day, though, he admits that he couldn't live anywhere else. "My wife and I have talked about it many times. But it makes us comfortable here."

After a lifetime of viewing the Village through the eyes of both an architect and a humanist, Polshek is amply qualified to pinpoint his affection for it. "It's really summed up for me in one word: scale," he says. "By that I mean the relationship of the buildings to the human body and the amount of detail that you can feel, touch, and absorb visually here. It's not absolutely unique because there are historic neighborhoods in other parts of the City. But as far as Manhattan is concerned, Greenwich Village is the home run."

West Village Original • Business

Danny Bensusan

January 2010

Photo: Danny Bensusan

Israeli-born Danny Bensusan opened The Blue Note on West Third Street in 1981. Featuring jazz greats as well as a host of younger artists, the club has become both an institution and a destination. In the ensuing years, he's opened up BB King's and the Highline Ballroom here in the city as well as Blue Note clubs in Japan and Milan. In addition, he owns a jazz recording label, Blue Note Live.

For entrepreneur Danny Bensusan, opening the Blue Note jazz club on West Third Street in 1981 was strictly a business decision.

"I always loved jazz music," he says. "But I didn't open the Blue Note for the love of jazz. I opened it because I thought the timing was right for it. Prior to that disco was the hot scene. It was the era of Studio 54 and such and that's where most people spent their entertainment money. In fact, when I bought the building on West Third Street it housed a disco called Gatsby's. Then disco started to fade, as people grew tired of it. I realized that live music was coming back. So I decided to go for the jazz even though I didn't know anything about it. However, I hired people who did."

"It wasn't easy in the beginning," he admits. "It took a year and half of losses until we figured out who the musicians were that would bring in the crowds. Most of our early musicians were good for a 100-seat room. However, I had 250 seats and I needed musicians who could fill them. It was difficult, but we managed with the help of people like Ray Brown, the bass player. He helped us to get Oscar Peterson and others of his caliber. Then we started looking for musicians who would attract not only the audience but the media as well. And we began presenting double bills, combining musicians who had not worked together in a long time. That attracted a lot of media and at the same time an audience. We got over the hump in our second and third year in business."

So what was Greenwich Village like in those days? "The Village was very, very alive when I first started," Bensusan remembers. "It seemed to be the only place for entertainment in New York City. Everything was down in the Village: clubs, cafes, restaurants. To walk late at night in the Village was like daytime anywhere else; it was always crowded. Then other areas in New York started to expand—such as Soho and Chelsea—and they took away some of the attraction of the Village."

"At the same time," he continues, "Community Board 2 did a lot of things that did not support businesses that wanted to bring good entertainment to the Village. So every corner turned into a Korean supermarket! That's because you don't need the Community Board to open one. You just do it. To open a nice club you need the approval of the Board, a liquor license, and a lot of things that the Board does not support. They couldn't care less if the Blue Note is in the Village or not. They don't care about real venues that bring true American art into the community."

Talking about some of the challenges that face the Village, Bensusan says, "The Village has always had its ups and downs. But it has one downfall: most of the places in it are small. When people started to move into Soho they opened up big galleries because it had big spaces. It was the same with Chelsea and the Meatpacking area, which also have huge spaces for clubs and galleries. You don't have that in the Village." Then he pauses to think for a moment. "Actually, if the places are big then NYU already took them!" he says, laughing.

Yet Bensusan feels, like most neighborhoods, the Village will bounce back as a nightlife destination. "Those small boutiques, clubs, and restaurants are going to come back to the Village," he predicts. As for the Blue Note itself, at this point it's an institution on the radar of tourists from around the globe. Part of that is because of the good relationships he's had with the artists who have appeared there over the years. "They loved the room," he says. "They loved the sound, and they had been treated well. The Blue Note was—and continues to be—their home away from home."

West Village Original • Business

Lisa Cannistraci

June 2013

Lisa Cannistraci is the owner of the bar Henrietta Hudson at the corner of Morton and Hudson Streets and is also vice-president of Marriage Equality USA's Board of Directors. Lisa has combined her love of activism with her business for over two decades now, and literally lives above her bar where "the ceiling touches my floor."

While growing up in Park Slope in the 60s, Lisa Cannistraci was attracted to activism at an early age. "My first foray into an election was when I was in 2nd grade," she recalls. "We had to pick a candidate for mayor and campaign for them. I picked John Lindsay and I went out at seven years old, talking to everybody. He won and I loved it! The civil rights movement had a big impact on me as well."

In 1985 Cannistraci started tending bar at the Cubbyhole and, when it closed, moved on to Kelly's Village West. "I was a bartender with a big following," she says. "At Kelly's I started doing a women's night on Sunday and it escalated into a huge event. One night, Minnie Rivera came in. Minnie was a veteran in the gay women's nightlife scene who owned a number of bars. She was an entrepreneur who saw something in me; how I was working the crowds and the room. She approached me to become her partner in reopening a new space in the old Cubbyhole. We named it Henrietta Hudson and opened on Halloween in 1991. Now we currently hold the record for being the longest consecutive running lesbian bar in the country."

Ironically, Cannistraci has found that as the gay rights movement moves forward, it has hurt her business a little. "I hate to say it," she admits. "But as people become more comfortable being out in the world, they have less of a reason to go to a lesbian venue." Yet Cannistraci plans to stay open "forever." "I mean that," she vows. "The bar is my passion and my love. What I love about it is that it's not only a business, but it's a business with a conscience. I can use Henrietta Hudson as a platform to reach out and do all the activism that I crave."

This activism really caught fire in 1992 when she helped launch "New York Boycott Colorado" after that state passed Amendment 2 and continues up to her current position with Marriage Equality USA. And while it's still a fight, things have gotten better. "In 1993, when we held the March on Washington, it was such a struggle to get our agenda across," she says. "But when I recently went to the Supreme Court as they were listening to the marriage equality arguments, we had the two best attorneys in the country advocating for us. From 1993 to 2013, it's such a different feeling about gay rights and marriage equality." What does she personally get from advocacy? "It's a beautiful feeling," she replies. "And you don't do it for that reason because you don't know what you're going to feel. But it fills me up. It really does."

When Cannistraci started working in the West Village there wasn't even a street light on the corner of Hudson and Morton. "There were no stop signs either," she says. "It was desolate. I could stand behind the bar for hours and not see anyone walk by. We were literally a destination location. And when I opened Henrietta's 20 years ago the Morton Street block association didn't want a lesbian bar. Now I'm on the community board and on the social services committee, helping local kids. It's so different now!"

Cannistraci is grateful to have landed in the West Village as both a business owner and a resident. "I feel really, really lucky to live here because it's my favorite place in the world," she says. "I've traveled extensively and there's nothing like it." According to her, this feeling is all the more reason to embrace change. "I don't really see the merit in not being a part of change. A lot of people have this grudge about the new people who are moving into the West Village. In my experience, though, they seem to be very invested in the community and they seem to care. Besides, instead of being pissed off at all the changes, why not do something about it? Things aren't going back to the way they were. Instead, let's put some energy into maintaining the waterfront, or plant trees, or raise money for a cause. Let's do something else to enhance the neighborhood and to make it ours."

West Village Original • Business

Bill O'Donnell

September 2012

Bill O'Donnell has owned the ever-popular Corner Bistro at Jane and West 4th Streets for the past 45 years. Born in Westwood, New Jersey in 1935, he also owns the building that the Bistro is in and keeps an office above the bar. You can see him there most mornings. Bill lives with his wife, Lorraine, on Bank Street.

Photo: Maggie Berkvist

In the summer of 1952, Bill O'Donnell worked as a bellboy on the SS *America*, doing three 18-day tours. "Among other ports, we hit Le Havre and Bremerhaven and it was my first exposure to Europe," he recalls. "I was sixteen and I looked about twelve and it was a real eye-opening experience. It was a lot of fun and an extraordinary amount of money for someone my age. The experience was 'broadening' is the best way to put it. It made my senior year difficult to finish because I went from that environment back to a Catholic high school!"

Was his tenure on the ship part of a grander life plan for O'Donnell? "I didn't have any plans then and I still don't!" he says, laughing. "I'm convinced that some days your life could be determined simply by which corner you turn. It's that random." He also claims to never have had a specific vocational drive or interest. "There were a lot of things I didn't want to do," he admits. "One was working in an office nine to five. I went back to college just to get an education and then I went back to sea for a while. I was toying with the idea of going to law school but that never materialized."

At this time there was a bar on Greenwich Avenue named Jack Barry's and the owner was looking for a weekend bartender. He asked O'Donnell to work until he figured out what he wanted to do. "I took that job and then a full-time bartending gig that opened up shortly after, never with the intention of continuing," O'Donnell says. "A few years later, one of the two owners of the Corner Bistro—his name was Curtis—wanted to sell his interest. I scrambled together some money from my brothers and me and that's how I began at the Corner Bistro. I took over 50% interest in February 1967 and ten years later bought the other 50%."

The bar had a minimal menu back then, so O'Donnell started serving hamburgers as the main attraction. "Some time around 1978 Mimi Sheraton, the food critic of the *New York Times*, came in and gave our hamburger a terrific review," he says. "That started the genesis of the hamburger business and it took on a life of its own. Newspapers and magazines started picking up on it. It became a big part of the Bistro and grew into what we've become today: a hamburger destination."

What was the bar scene like back then? "It was much different," says O'Donnell. "It was a mixed clientele and an eclectic crowd. You had neighborhood people, beatniks, some longshoreman, and tourists. You also had the aspiring actors, writers, poets and the intellectual types. So it was a collision of cultures and sometimes it didn't mix so well! There seemed to be a lot more drinking then. Today you can't do anything in a bar because as soon as someone belches too loudly people are on their cell phones!" He laughs, and continues. "I think the bar scene in general is much more peaceful than it was years ago."

In addition, the gentrification of the Village, particularly in the last ten years, has changed his clientele dramatically. "The crowd has gotten a lot younger," O'Donnell says. "We have a group of standby older people that come late in the afternoon. We also do a lot of tourist business during the day as well. But at nighttime it's all young people. I feel like Methusaleh if I go in at night. Most people are in their late twenties or early thirties. They're that young!"

For a fellow who started out with no clear life plan, it turns out that O'Donnell ended up doing pretty well after all. "I do take some pride in the fact that the Bistro is so successful," he admits. "It means I've just hung in for such a length of time. I wasn't an innovator of any sort. I just persevered. And if you hang around long enough, good things can happen. The Bistro still represents something of the past and people like that. It's reminiscent of old New York and it's maintained its integrity."

West Village Original • Business

Nicky Perry

October 2011

Photo: Maggie Berkvist

London native Nicky Perry is owner of Tea & Sympathy on Greenwich Avenue for over twenty years. In addition to the restaurant, she also owns Carry On Tea & Sympathy, the shop next door that sells all things British. A firm believer in giving back to the community, Perry is also very active in the West Village affairs, including trying to get another hospital to replace the now-closed St. Vincent's.

As a girl growing up in London, Nicky Perry felt destined to live in New York. "I knew I belonged here years before I came," she says. "Every time I heard the words 'New York' my ears would prick up. I couldn't hear enough about it. My mum brought me here for my 21st birthday for a week and then—eight months later—I came back on my own with $200 in my pockets. That was 1981. $200 wouldn't buy you dinner today! But there was no turning back for me."

The first year she was in New York, Perry went out to dinner with a friend who complained that there were no English restaurants here and she couldn't get a good cup of tea. "That's when the light bulb went off in my head and I was obsessed," she says. "I knew I wanted to open a tea shop, what it would look like, and what I would sell. So I started working in restaurants where I gained experience. By the time I was 31—and just six months after I got my green card—my father gave me £10,000 to open the restaurant. My partner matched the money, my brother renovated it, a friend of mine decorated it, and on December 23, 1990 we opened Tea & Sympathy."

Happily, the restaurant is still open. This constitutes a bit of a miracle in a neighborhood that has seen most of its long-time restaurants and shops close up. Perry thinks much of her restaurant's longevity is due to its uniqueness. "I consider myself very lucky because I'm doing what no one else is doing," she says. "I have a customer base that stretches far and wide. I'm also a small restaurant so that helps. I guess you could call me one of the St. Vincent's Hospital survivors."

This last observation leads Perry to expound on an issue that is very close to her heart: the closing of St. Vincent's. "I am absolutely apoplectic about that hospital closing," she cries. "It's unconscionable! This is the third most expensive zip code in America and this is what happens to us? How can we be living in a society where condos are more important than people's health? It's beyond belief. That hospital was this entire neighborhood's livelihood and now businesses are gone and doctors are gone."

Continuing in this vein, she compares what's happened to the West Village in general as "living in a world of Pacman." "All the amazing little business that have been here for years have just been eaten up," she explains. "We're the dots and the corporations are the men eating us all alive. It's like Starbucks or Ralph Lauren say, 'Let's munch this block up!' This raises commercial rents to ridiculous heights, which in turn stifles any artistic expression or risk taking. That's because if you go into a space that costs $20,000 a month to rent, you have to go into it with a corporate attitude. This will destroy us all. And it will destroy the American dream. You can't come here with $200 in your pocket and a fabulous idea anymore."

When asked if she thinks there's any hope for the West Village, Perry takes a breath. "I think there is hope, yes," she says finally. "I think there always has to be hope. Things change all the time and you never know what's going to happen tomorrow. It's sad and it's disappointing what's happening in the West Village today, but it doesn't necessarily mean it's going to stay that way. Nothing in life does."

And for the time being, she can proudly point to her restaurant and it's iconic status in the community. "I just love every minute of the business," she confesses. "I love that it's different all the time. You never know what's going to happen next or who's going to walk through the door. No day is the same and the people you meet are amazing, especially in this neighborhood. People talk to each other here. It's still very neighborly, which is very British. The West Village is probably the closest to anything you'd find in England, and certainly London."

West Village Original • Business

Stephanie Phelan

August 2012

Photo: Maggie Berkvist

WestView's former Creative Director, Stephanie Phelan has been a neighborhood resident for 33 years. Throughout a varied career that has encompassed modeling, graphic design, dog portraitist, auxiliary police officer, and blogger, one thing has remained constant: her commitment to the community. Her work can be viewed at www.phelandogart.com.

When she was a girl growing up in Montclair, New Jersey, Stephanie Phelan's first love was painting and thanks to an uncle who built her a studio, she had ample opportunity to practice the art. "I was considered a prodigy and I sold all my paintings when I was a kid," she says. "They thought I would go on to become a fine artist but I didn't want that life. I wanted to be a blonde, busty cheerleader. I wanted to be normal!" she continues, laughing. "Needless to say, it never happened."

After a year-and-a-half of college, Phelan moved to New York in 1965 and got a job at the advertising agency Doyle Dane Bernbach. "I was an administrative assistant and an art buyer," she recalls. "They were wonderful to me. I met all kinds of people and a lot of photographers who came in would say, 'We want her to become a model.' I was in a couple of magazine spreads but it wasn't much, believe me. I just wasn't suited for it. I didn't have the personality. But it was fun for about six months to have people introduce me as a model." However, what Phelan did learn was graphic design, a skill that has steadily supported her over the years, including a period when she lived on Martha's Vineyard and worked as a designer for the local Chamber of Commerce. She moved back to Manhattan for good in 1979.

When she was nearing 40 and feeling she needed a backup career, Phelan went back to painting. Only this time it was what she calls "primitive miniatures" of dogs. "It was kind of a natural because I love dogs and I love icons," she says. "I found little pieces of wood on the street and bought enamel paint sets. I did them a little tongue in cheek as icons but I really feel that our dogs are something spiritual for us." Why the miniature format? "Part of what prompts my creative endeavors is a feeling that there's a void in a certain area. At the time I started doing dog portraits, there were just traditional oil portraits. So my small icons just felt right and people really loved them."

In keeping with her sense of community, one of Phelan's proudest achievements was becoming an Auxiliary Police officer in 1981. "I joined the Sixth Precinct on West 10th Street," she says. "I went into training, got my shield and that was that. It was wonderful. I became even more attached to the neighborhood and I learned a lot about people. You don't have to be tough all the time, just some times. Mostly you're just being genial. I gained a great deal of self-confidence and my husband was very supportive of it even though we split up a year or two later."

Not surprisingly, for someone who has spent so much time on the streets of the West Village, Phelan has had a bird's eye view of the changes over the years. "I think most people see it as changing a lot," she says. "It's gotten safer. It's gotten a little less interesting in a lot of ways, too. It's not so much of a Pinko liberal place anymore." She laughs. "Although, my attitude towards that has changed too," she continues. "On that end of things I'm more conservative and I do believe in law enforcement and I believe that people objecting to things like a fence around Washington Square Park isn't reasonable. We want things to be clean, safe and pleasant and there has to be some rules."

It also feels like the West Village has become a tighter neighborhood as well to Phelan. "It might just be my personal experience of having a dog, living in my amazing building, and being on the police force," she says. "But you know everybody. You can't walk down the street without saying hello to twenty people. You feel people are there for you and I'm there for them. The changes to the neighborhood haven't seemed so bad to me because I find my street is still safe and pretty and friendly. This is where my community is. I love living in the Village! I can't tell you…it just brings tears to my eyes."

West Village Original • Business

Billy Romp
December 2009

Photo: Maggie Berkvist

Since 1988 Vermonter Billy Romp and his family have been selling Christmas trees at the corner of Jane Street and Eighth Avenue, forging lifelong friendships with neighborhood residents through the years. Their story has been immortalized in a book entitled "Christmas on Jane Street" by Romp and Wanda Urbanska and is available for purchase at the stand.

For Billy Romp and his family, their annual pilgrimage to the West Village to sell Christmas trees is framed around a desire to see old friends, make new ones, and—above all—offer the best customer service in town. "Everybody's got nice trees on the corner," Romp says. "If we're going to distinguish ourselves, it's with our retail excellence and customer service. We like to think that no one will go further than us. I may look like a hick out there, but we treat this as a serious business."

Born in upstate Troy, Romp moved to Vermont in the 1970s "with all the other back-to-the-land hippies." And how did the current tradition get started? "My wife Patti and I were looking for another thing to add to our annual income," Romp recalls. "We heard of a friend who had gone down to New York City to sell trees and made better money than by doing it in Vermont. Then we talked to other people who had done it, including a tree wholesaler who mentioned that Jane Street was available. My knowledge of Greenwich Village was pretty slim then. All I knew is that it had gay people and actors! So we came down, expecting nothing. We just hoped we could survive and make a few dollars."

So what's it been like? "It's been life-changing," Romp enthuses. "Part of my whole identity now is wrapped up with the fact that I've spent almost 10% of my life in Greenwich Village. The relationships

I have with the people I've met down here are the most important part of the whole thing. The money is great and the experience is great. But it's the people I've befriended that have made the biggest difference in my life. I can't think of another mechanism where we could've met such a broad range of people so different from ourselves"

As someone who only visits yearly, Romp is in a particularly good position to observe changes to the neighborhood. "The gentrification is really obvious to me," he says. "I'm on the street and I can see the changes right away. When we first came here, the transvestites and hookers from the meat market would spill over into the neighborhood. I saw crack vials on the corner of Jane Street those first couple of years. I saw violence as well. And I've seen what everyone else has seen: the general cleaning up of the neighborhood."

Romp continues. "I could talk about the physical changes but I also want to emphasize that there are a lot of people walking their dogs who were here in 1988. However, many of them worry that they will have to leave one day because they can't afford the area anymore, particularly the renters. A lot of them are afraid of their landlord because they know that he wants them to leave."

When asked what he thinks some of the challenges facing the West Village these days are, Romp deliberates for a moment. "I think it would be the challenge of cohesiveness," he ventures. "There are a few people who are really interested in keeping the community together. However, I fear these activists are smaller in number than they used to be so it seems that the same people are carrying the load. I just hope it's a big enough number to keep this neighborhood's character preserved. In my opinion, there's nothing at all like the West Village."

It's that character that fosters the special ties Romp has with his customers, some of them generational now. "There's one particular family that I've been delivering a tree to and setting it up for 22 years," he relays. "The family's little girl that I met 22 years ago now has her own apartment on Jane Street and her own baby, and I'm setting up their tree as well. If things go as planned, my sons will be setting up the tree for her little girl when I'm an old man. There's a wonderful continuity to this relationship with our clients. They treasure it. I treasure it. You couldn't ever replace it."

West Village Original • Business

David Maurice Sharp

April 2015

Photo: Maggie Berkvist

Actor, dancer, choreographer, and financial advisor David Maurice Sharp was born in Avonmore, Pennsylvania. His book "The Thriving Artist: Saving and Investing for Performers and Artists" was recently published by Focus Press For the past seven years, he has also been giving free investing workshops at HB Studio on Bank Street.

"If I had known back in the day the kind of road I would go on I would have found it very interesting," says David Sharp, with a certain amount of understatement. When he came to New York in 1980, it was to study acting and dancing at NYU's Tisch School of the Arts. And yet it was going to work for a Wall Street firm that changed the trajectory of his life. "All these disparate elements of my life have kind of gelled together now," he says. "When I was doing the Wall Street stuff I thought it had nothing to do with my creative life—except financially—and vice versa. But I love that both careers helped get me to this point."

It all started around 1987 when Sharp was trying to figure out how to make money until his next gig came along and he signed onto a temp agency. "The first place they sent me was a proxy solicitor on Wall Street," he says. "They hired me as a temp but then they started sending me out on business trips. One day said they wanted to hire me directly. I had no intention of giving up dance, but they asked if I could give them 20 hours a week. I ended up doing just that and I was with that firm for almost 13 years! They always let me pursue my artistic endeavors whether I was on tour, attending classes, or in rehearsal."

"At the same time I learned about stock and bonds," he continues. "Friends in the arts began asking me to explain to them the intricacies of investing so we formed a group called The Thriving Artists Investment

Club. We paid dues of $25 a month. We pooled these dues and invested them in securities, eventually forming a partnership. The club was in existence for just under ten years and we made over a 40% profit when we cashed out. We did pretty well for a bunch of artists!"

Sharp declares the best thing about what he does is giving artists the ability to feel like they can take control of their finances. He doesn't blame them for their initial reservations, though. "No one is ever really taught investing," he says. "If you haven't been exposed, it's scary. It's like learning a different language. But I think a lot of the traits that artists have make them good at finance. For example, their creativity: they're able to think in ways that can be very useful when looking for investments. I also think the discipline they have is essential. Artists understand the notion that hard work needs to be put in to achieve results, whether they're performing or investing."

Sharp moved into the West Village almost 25 years ago. "When I was at NYU and living in the dorm on Fifth Avenue and Tenth Street, I remember thinking that this might be the best address I would ever have in New York!" he says laughing. "But then I got into this apartment on Bleecker Street. I sublet it the first few years and I bought it in the late 90s. Before I did, though, I was terrified. I didn't know how I was going to pay my mortgage. But my father was very instrumental, saying 'You need to buy it because it will make a big difference in your life.' Thank goodness he did!"

Since then, Sharp has watched as the neighborhood has changed dramatically. "Bleecker Street in particular is almost unrecognizable," he says. "It used to be all these unique stores and restaurants. Do you remember when Judith Stiles had her pottery shop here? I loved taking people there. I think all of my sisters have a piece of hers, which they bought when visiting. Those kinds of places I really miss. Now Bleecker has become the Rodeo Drive of New York!"

And yet he's pragmatic about the change as well. "Change happens!" he admits. "What I love about the West Village is that in such a big, busy city it's maintained a sense of identity, of being it's own neighborhood. Despite the changes that have happened here I think it's held on to that quality. It's still a wonderful neighborhood. It's just different."

West Village Original • Business

Three Lives & Company

July 2014

Photo: Maggie Berkvist

This installment of West Village Originals is doing something different: focusing on a longtime neighborhood business instead of a particular resident. Of course, the venerable bookstore Three Lives & Company can't speak for itself, so we spoke to current owner, California-born Toby Cox. Toby lives in Fort Greene, Brooklyn and travels into Manhattan every day to manage the store.

In 1978, at the corner of Seventh Avenue and Tenth Street in the West Village, three women opened a bookstore called Three Lives and Company. A few years later the shop—whose name is a riff on Gertrude Stein's first novel *Three Lives*—moved a block away to the corner of 10th Street and Waverly Place where it remains to this day.

Jump to 1997, when Providence bookseller Toby Cox was wandering this neighborhood, stumbled upon a little corner bookshop, and opened the door. "I probably gasped," Cox says. "I thought, 'This is the store I would have!' I was so enchanted. The space that those three women created was magical. It really celebrated the book." Six months later, Cox moved to New York (Brooklyn, to be exact) to work in marketing for Random House. He made his way back to the Three Lives & Company, met the owners—now down to two, named Jill and Jenny—and became friendly with them. "I would pass through here at least once a month and touch the books," he says. "It was one of those places that acted like a magnet, drawing me back time after time."

Three years later, Cox looked up the ladder of the publishing business and decided it wasn't where he wanted to spend his life. "I wanted to be at the end where the book meets the public," he says. "I realized the book selling is truly what I love to do. One night I was in here with Jill and just as an aside I asked her, 'Do you guys want a partner?' Right at that time she and Jenny were deciding to retire and I was actually someone they wanted to approach about taking over the shop. It was this nice moment of serendipity." Eventually Cox worked out the transfer and took ownership in February of 2001.

What's it like having a business in the West Village? "It's an amazing neighborhood," Cox admits. "People are so supportive of not just their little independent bookshop, but all of the other shops as well. There's a very strong sense here about what makes their neighborhood special and a real community; it's not just the residents, the beautiful architecture, and the tree-lined streets but also the health of those commercial enterprises that are part of that neighborhood." It's this sense of community that makes Cox feel lucky to be a part of this store. "We have people who come into the shop four or five times a week," he continues. "It's really just a place for them stop and talk about the weather or the news or the last book they loved. Or bring their dog by to get a biscuit. It's that kind of thing. I feel like, yes, I'm the owner. But in a sense I'm just the caretaker of Three Lives and it's my position to maintain this space for the community."

Cox feels that the independent bookstores have weathered three storms—chains, Amazon, and e-readers—and they've settled down somewhat. "There is a place for the smaller, well-curated, dedicated-to-community and nimble little bookshop now," he says. "It's not uncommon for me to say, 'I know who would like this book.' I think our customers and the interactions we have with them are definitely the key to this bookstore's longevity. People tell me where all the other bookshops were in this neighborhood before my time and it makes me happy that we're still here."

When asked if Three Lives & Company could exist in any other part of New York, Cox makes the distinction. "I think a 650 square foot bookshop could exist in many places in the City," he says. "As for the personality that is Three Lives & Company on the corner of Waverly and West Tenth Street, no. That's very specific to the West Village. Of course, New York City is full of passionate, engaged, and curious readers. But I don't think you could duplicate the shop—the full essence of it if you will—anywhere else in town. It just wouldn't be the same."

West Village Original • Business

Arnold S. Warwick

July 2009

Arnold S. Warwick—born in Crown Heights, Brooklyn in 1931—founded an eponymous real estate management and brokerage company in Greenwich Village in 1963, and is still its chief executive. A longtime resident of Commerce Street, he and his wife Jane raised three children there. Warwick is also president of the Board of Directors of Westbeth, which he says, "Makes my retirement years interesting."

When Arnold S. Warwick moved to Greenwich Village in the mid-1950s, rents were modest—to say the least—by today's standards. "We were on Carmine Street and the rent was $11 a month," he recollects. "After that, we moved to a posh place on Jones Street that actually had a toilet in the apartment. That one rented for $17 a month." Then he laughs. "These aren't the prices of sandwiches, mind you. These are the actual rents we paid back then!"

Warwick's subsequent move from renter to building manager wasn't by way of his obstetrician father or schoolteacher mother, but rather through longtime Village resident and real estate agent Charles Keith. "Charlie was an interesting man," Warwick recalls. "He was wounded three times in Spain between 1937 and 1939. He also spent thirteen months in a Fascist prison there. Then he came to the Village, became a house painter, opened a real estate office, and rented me an apartment. At that point I was selling tickets at the Cherry Lane Theatre and he asked me if I wanted to work in his office part time. So I worked there from noon to four or five and then went to the theatre to sell tickets." Keith's business was called Apartment Rentals Service, on West 8th Street. It was right next to the old Marlton Hotel. "We would hang out the window and watch all the people going into the hotel for afternoon assignations," Warwick admits.

Eventually Warwick had to go elsewhere because Keith's partner came back from Europe and "She couldn't stand anyone else in the office," he says. "So Charlie got me a job at Hanfield & Bell, also on 8th Street. They subsequently merged with another firm, at which point I was let go and opened my own management office. That was 1963 and I've been on my own ever since."

Among several anecdotes as a building manager, Warwick recounts the time he was hired to move John Cage and Merce Cunningham, who lived together at 107 Bank Street. "The building they lived in was owned by a woman named Rose Slivka," he says. "She was very involved in the Craft movement. She hired me to get them to move because she wanted to do something with the building. It wasn't difficult or nasty or one of those landlord/tenant things. In fact, the two men were delighted to move and bought a space in a loft building over on Sixth Avenue. After I got them to leave, Rose promptly fired me."

When asked what some of the biggest changes he's witnessed over the years in the West Village are, Warwick replies, "The new construction and the renovations of older buildings. And it's really hard to weigh things like that. In some instances it's good, and some bad. When they took dreadful slum-like buildings down, that was advantageous. When they took perfectly good buildings down because they wanted the land, then no. So it varies from spot to spot." While there hasn't been a huge amount of new construction in the West Village, he says there have been lots of conversions and renovations of older buildings. "When I first moved to the Village, the banks wouldn't even look at a loan west of Seventh Avenue! However, as the loft movement began to blossom, developers started buying warehouses in the West Village and converting them. That development west of Seventh Avenue was amazing and it threw a lot of people into the area that might not have been able to fit in it otherwise."

After a half-century of residence, Warwick's favorite aspects of living in the neighborhood are, "Walking to work and all the restaurants that are available for lunch." In addition, he claims that it was a terrific place to raise kids. Which brings him to what he thinks is one of the biggest challenges facing the West Village today. "It's the necessity for people to find places for their children to go to school," he says. "The shortage of schools in this neighborhood is definitely a problem. I certainly don't think we have a shortage of dog walkers. Or, luckily, of very pretty women either." He laughs. "All I've got left are my eyeballs!"

> *I'm not one of those people who think that everything great happened in the past. I still feel this neighborhood is exciting. That's because people who march to a different drummer come to the Village. They always will.*
>
> —David Rothenberg

West Village Original • Community Activism

Keen Berger
August 2014

Photo: Maggie Berkvist

Author and educator Kathleen Stassen Berger was born in Minnesota in 1942 while her father was Governor. For over three decades, Berger has taught human development to a diverse student body at Bronx Community College as well as writing such bestselling textbooks as "Invitation to the Life Span." A West Village resident since 1968, Keen and her husband raised their four daughters here.

For Keen Berger, observing people has been a lifelong fascination. "My husband Martin was many wonderful things, among them an amateur gardener," she relates. "One time he excitedly called me to the back yard to look at a flower that had just bloomed. However, I looked at the wrong flower and he said, "I grow beauty for you and you don't even notice it!"" She laughs. "But what I've always noticed is what people are doing and why they're doing it. That's where my eyes and my thoughts go. That's what developmental psychologists do."

What drew Berger to this particular field? "Two things," she replies. "One is that I had some gifted teachers who were developmental psychologists. And the same year I started my PhD, I had my first child. So both personally and professionally I became captivated by the whole process of development. Of course, developmental psychology is 'life span' psychology so it's about adults, too. Everybody is constantly developing and to me that's riveting. I walk down the street and I look at people, or I sit on the subway and I look at families. I'm fascinated by how they act, what they do and say, and how they move and interact with each other." She has the same passion for how communities function and work to make themselves better. "That passion was certainly in my family growing up," Berger says. "And that's what drew me to my husband. We were both in the civil rights movement back in the day. It made a lot of sense, working for justice for all people."

When Berger and her husband started having children they were living on Bedford Street and she assumed they would have to move to the suburbs. "But Martin said, 'No, we can do it here,'" she recalls. "That surprised me, but it turned out to be a great place to raise children and they had a wonderful upbringing. When our daughter Rachel returned from her first semester at college in Maine, she said, 'Mom, you protected me too much. I never knew there was so much homophobia or sexism in the world!'" Berger laughs. "That's symbolic of growing up in the Village. You're much more likely to understand people of all different backgrounds and appreciate them."

Having lived here for such a long time, what does Berger consider the biggest change to the neighborhood? "The saddest part is that it has become much more elite," Berger observes. "Many wealthy people have come in and many of the artistic types have moved out, especially the young. Now the people who live here are a very different demographic." That said, she does consider the possibility that things could always change again. "Social change is very interesting and it's hard to predict. I don't expect things to go in a linear direction here and I expect there will be some surprises. I'm not sure what they will be, though. Perhaps one day my kids—who can only afford Brooklyn now—will be able to move back to the Village!"

In the meantime, Berger relishes her life here. "I run up and down Hudson Park, I love the High Line, and I'm a member of Judson Memorial Church," Berger says. "And of course I like shopping in some of the old stores. I still get candy at Lilac." There's also the sense of community here that sustains her. "I know a lot of people and have a lot of neighbors, so personally I have a great sense of community. There's a political community here as well. And lastly, because of my profession, I write and think about growing old and the West Village is a wonderful place for that. It's a safe area where you can walk to all kinds of stores at all hours, and there are numerous opportunities for older people. I think it's a great place to raise children as I did, but it's also a great place to grow old."

West Village Original • Community Activism

Andrew Berman

September 2020

Andrew Berman has been Executive Director of Village Preservation (formerly GVSHP) since 2002. Berman was born in the Bronx and grew up in Co-Op City. In 2013, he was named to the Vanity Fair "Hall of Fame" for his preservation work. Berman attended Bronx High School of Science and then Wesleyan University, where he received a degree in Art History with a focus on architecture.

Growing up in the Bronx, Andrew Berman became aware at an early age of the perils of big public projects. "My mother's family lived in one of the first apartment buildings demolished by Robert Moses to make way for the Cross Bronx Expressway," he says. "I heard a lot about that. There was definitely a consciousness about how that and other projects by Moses destroyed neighborhoods. My father was a hardware salesman who spent his days driving throughout the five boroughs and sometimes I would go with him. He had a very broad knowledge of the City: its different areas, what they were like, who lived there, and how they had changed. I think I absorbed a lot of that from him and, no doubt, my parents influenced my interest in preservation."

It wasn't long after college that Berman started an eight-year tenure with New York politician Tom Duane, who represented Greenwich Village, among other neighborhoods. It was, he admits, experience that turned out to be "incredibly useful" in his current position. "In order to be successful in New York City—in terms of historical preservation—you have to bring together both knowledge and history of the built environment," he says. "You also need to be effective at community organizing and understand how the levers of government affect these issues. You could have the most wonderfully argued and researched proposal for landmarking a building, but if you don't know how to organize people to lobby for it or understand how the system works in terms of the decision-making process, you're not likely to be successful."

Last year, GVSHP became Village Preservation to better reflect its mission. "We shortened and broadened the name to reflect the fact that we serve Greenwich Village and the East Village too," Berman explains. "And because our mission now extends beyond what you would traditionally call historical preservation to small business and cultural institution preservation as well. It was kind of an organic extension because these were things we cared about." As to his leadership of Village Preservation, Berman claims that it's a "dream job." "I actually get to do something that I love as my job and as the main focus of my professional life," he says. "I find the history, architecture, and culture of our neighborhoods to be wonderful. And I get to work with a really engaged community that cares about things."

Since this is *WestView*, we encouraged Berman to express any special feelings about our neighborhood in particular. "I love the West Village," he readily admits. "It remains one of the most unique, charming, magical places not just in New York, but in the world. It faces incredible challenges, though, from enormous development pressure to the fact that it's become so incredibly expensive. I guess that's a validation that it is so desirable, which is what we've fought for. But you also don't want it to become a place that doesn't remain accessible to the broader world. I think many of the new residents, as much as the old, feel that way too. No one is moving here because they want to be barricaded from the rest of the world. They move here because there's a community that's a mixture of people, activities, places to shop, and things to do and learn."

Does Berman feel the influx of monied residents into the Village will allow it to stay true to what makes it such a special place? "Certainly some people of great means who move into the neighborhood aren't really invested in the wonderful qualities of the community," he says. "And then there are those who very much are. Regarding preservation, though, there can be good and bad outcomes from the investment of money and there can be good and bad outcomes from the lack of money. I don't think money is by itself either the problem or the solution. Rather, it's how it's used. The West Village has always been about a sense of community. Maintaining this, along with a level of diversity, is definitely important to the soul of the neighborhood."

West Village Original • Community Activism

Frederic Block

January 2016

Photo: Maggie Berkvist

Frederic Block is senior judge of the United States District Court for the Eastern District of New York. Born in Brooklyn in 1934 and raised in Manhattan, he has presided over high-profile cases involving the Crown Heights riots, Kitty Genovese, and mob boss Peter Gotti. Block moved to the West Village in 1994 and is the author of "Disrobed: An Inside Look at the Life and Work of a Federal Trial Judge."

Although he was born in Brooklyn, Frederic Block claims his father did "a wonderful thing" by moving the family to Manhattan when he was nine years old. "We lived at 16 West 72nd Street, across from the New York Historical Society," he recalls. "It was a great place to be raised from the years of 8 to 18. We used to play stickball in the street and stoop ball on the steps of the Museum of Natural History. That was our playground."

According to Block, he got into law by a process of elimination. "When I barely passed the Regents physics exam in high school I concluded I was not going to be another Albert Einstein," he says ruefully. "So I gravitated to other things. I was always interested in law and I passed the bar in 1959. I wish I could say 1960, it sounds more modern!" He laughs. "But the law keeps your mind very active. You can graduate when I did and still be practicing now. I think there's a correlation to keeping your mind stimulated and enhancing the quality of your life."

What is it about the law that appeals to Block? "For me, the law is an engine of social change," he replies. "When people think of law they think mostly of social issues: abortion, same-sex marriage, etc. Those were all litigated using the law to address them. This is not the product of business, trust, or real estate lawyers by the way. While I respect lawyers of every stripe, I believe what litigators do with the law means the most to people. I think litigators are comparable to what heart surgeons are in medicine."

Block's well-received memoir—*Disrobed: An Inside Look at the Life and Work of a Federal Trial Judge*—was published a few years ago. "I find that most people don't have a clue about the judiciary," he says, explaining that this behind-the-scenes account of his career as a judge was a way to cast some light on it. "Judges have knowledge and experience," he continues. "We have it within our power to educate people about what the judicial process is all about. I wrote the book to reach out to the public in non-academic language and I thought people would enjoy it." There's another side to his profession that the public doesn't hear about. "We have a whole range of judges that have creative talents," Block says by way of explanation. "I'm a jazz pianist myself. I also wrote a musical called *Professionally Speaking*, a send-up about lawyers, doctors, and teachers that had a brief run off-Broadway back in the 80s. I dabble in writing music, which is my hobby. And I'm writing my second book, *Law and Disorder*. It's a pun. I fictionalize the DA race in Brooklyn when Ken Thompson unseated Charles Hynes."

When Block was appointed judge in 1994 he could have lived any place in the metropolitan area but he chose the West Village. "It appealed to me," he says. "The cultural mix and the character of the place. It has a nice feel to it in terms of the population, the openness, and the whole basic environment."

As for the changes he's seen in the interim, some are positive and some worrisome. "I like the way the Hudson River Park has evolved," he says. "When I moved here there was nothing: no grass, no median, and no parkland. Now it's magnificent! On the other hand, I'm looking at a building going up on my street and while it's attractive, it's going to start at $3,000 a square foot! I'm not so sure that's a healthy thing. It only invites a very small group of people into the neighborhood: those who have millions and millions of dollars. I'm afraid it's going to affect the diversity of the Village in the long term and that bothers me a little bit."

And yet he must admit that the West Village encourages—in his own words—his "eclectic personality." "Oh yes," Block responds. "I feel I'm a real dilettante. It's fortunate that you can have all these interests, especially as you get older. You feel blessed to be that type of person and in a neighborhood that supports it."

West Village Original • Community Activism

Carmen Grange

September 2018

Dr. Carmen Grange was born in 1922 in Colón, Panama to Jamaican parents working in the Canal Zone. Grange studied pre-med at Trinity College in Dublin and returned to the USA to do her residency, eventually opening a practice on West 13th Street. A resident of Charles Street since 1964, she was also Medical Director at Greenwich House, and affiliated with Beekman Downtown Hospital.

"I wanted to be a doctor and nothing would stop me," says Carmen Grange, referring to the time when she was a young girl in Jamaica. "I was born in Panama but my parents separated when I was young and I was sent to Jamaica to live with my grandmother. She was a midwife and I would accompany her when she did her work. That's why I wanted to do medicine from an early age."

Grange was to discover that—for various reasons—it wasn't going to be easy to attain her dream. "Sometimes it was the issue of my being a woman and sometimes because I was a woman of color," she says. "It took some time but I just persevered. I was attending college in Jamaica but I couldn't get into pre-med there. They suggested that I go into social work, instead! So I applied to Trinity College in Dublin and they accepted me. That was in 1959 and I was there for about five years." What was that experience like? "I felt welcomed in Dublin," she replies. "I had no problem being a woman of color studying medicine. It was nice, too, because there were people from all over the world doing the same thing. After I finished, I came back to the USA to do my residency."

When Grange started her own practice—eventually opening an office on West 13th Street—she focused on internal medicine. "I liked internal medicine because I liked taking care of people with my hands," she says. "I took care of patients of all colors. You have to like what you're doing, which I always did." Did she ever again face the kind of resistance she did while trying to get into medical school? "No. Once you're a doctor—woman or man—you're a doctor," she says with a shrug. "And I don't really miss it because I'm so old now. People still ask me questions that I'm able to answer, though."

Grange never married even though she did have the opportunity while in Dublin. "I refused to get married because the man was Danish and I didn't want to move to Denmark," she says, smiling. "I wanted to come back to America. However, I've had a wonderful, intellectual family life thanks to my 16 nieces and nephews who are still around me. I helped educate them all. I spent all my money on them and it was worth it. Today they're lawyers, doctors, and even a veterinarian. What was the point of making all that money if I didn't spend it on them?"

Grange moved into her high-rise on Charles Street in 1964, the year it was built. "I had family connections with this part of the world from way back when," she says. "When I moved in I used to have a great view of both the East River and the Hudson River. Of course, it's changed a lot but I still I like the West Village. I did a lot here because I was always an active person. I love the local restaurants, too: Baby Brasa, Morandi—in my building—and the Riviera Café, which is gone now."

These days Dr. Grange finds herself homebound due to suffering a heart attack a few years ago. But she maintains her connection to family and her longtime church, St. John's in the Village. "I've had a good and busy life," she says. "I especially loved all the traveling because in those days it was so nice. Not like today, which is so complicated. As a doctor I went to meetings and conferences all over the world and I met a lot of interesting people. It's a big, varied world and Thank God for it. My grandmother used to say, 'If you can't do any good, at least don't do any evil!' I've never forgotten those words and they're still true."

West Village Original • Community Activism

David Gruber

September 2009

David Gruber enjoys a lengthy resume of membership in community organizations, including president of the Carmine Street Block Association, president of the South Village Landmark Association, and chairman of the Arts and Institutions Committee for Community Board 2. He has lived with his wife Helen, a graphic designer, on Carmine Street for thirty years.

For Manhattan-born David Gruber, it took a noisy restaurant to get him started in community service. "I had spent my life not really being involved," he admits. "We had lived on Carmine Street for years when this restaurant opened and installed loudspeakers that went into the back courtyard, which was residential. We complained about it and we were ignored. So I organized the Carmine Street Courtyard Organization, which included the seven families living there. We went to the community board and protested the restaurant's application for a sidewalk license."

The community board ruled in the residents' favor. However, the restaurant then approached another City agency, which did, in fact, grant them a license. This made Gruber really angry. "I then went to the full board meeting," he recalls. "I asked them just what the point was of the board turning down the restaurant's request, only to be ignored by another agency? At that time, Audrey Leeds was the chair of the sidewalk committee and said, 'So come and join the committee as a public member.' And I did."

Gruber continues. "At the time, maybe 10, 12 years ago, the city's agencies did what they wanted. We repeatedly turned down liquor licenses and they routinely overturned our decisions. But I got to learn the system and, given my background with the planning commission, I became a member of the zoning committee. Over time, Community

Board 2 became very focused. And now, community boards in general have become very empowered in this city. You have people on the boards that really know their stuff. Politicians listen. Council members listen. The planning commission listens. We resonate much more with the city agencies."

How has the Village changed since he first moved in? "It's become much more of an area for nightlife," Gruber observes. "People come to the Village and think they can raise hell because there's no community. That isn't true, but the presence of lots of bars and certain stores such as the porn shops and tattoo parlors on lower Sixth Avenue doesn't help." He does offer a note of conciliation. "The Community Board is not really against anything, we're just against excess," Gruber explains. "That's what people don't realize: how citizens like myself and hundreds of others are preserving this neighborhood for the generations that come after us. Hopefully they'll know about the work we put in."

One thing Gruber is proudest of is his effort to rehabilitate Father Demo Square at Sixth Avenue and Carmine Street. "That's almost my legacy," he says. "Back in 2000, the park was filthy. It was open all night, there were screaming fights, and homeless people were living in it, draping their blankets over the benches or sleeping in cardboard boxes. It was a very hostile environment and it no longer functioned as a neighborhood park." So Gruber formed the Friends of Father Demo to lobby for change. It was a long fight, but they prevailed. "Now it's a peaceful park that closes at midnight," he says with pride. "I think it's the jewel in the crown of New York parks. Per square foot we're one of the most highly used parks in the city. It's working, and the community—senior citizens, kids, tourists—is actually using it."

Citing one of the biggest challenges facing the Village today, Gruber takes the developers to task. "They come into the far West Village with its beautiful old buildings and water views and say, 'We love it here. Let's see how we can kill it!'" He laughs. "We're under siege because we have this beautiful community that's different from any other neighborhood in Manhattan and developers come in and put up buildings totally out of scale. So the test is to keep this an historic part of New York. Our mandate here is not to say there can't be change, but that it needs to be respectful of the history and scale of the West Village. That's the challenge for me—and all of us—moving forward."

West Village Original • Community Activism

Ralph Lee
March 2014

Photo: Maggie Berkvist

Ralph Lee is the founder of the Village Halloween Parade. Born in Middlebury, Vermont in 1935, he is a master mask-maker and currently artistic director of The Mettawee River Theatre Company, which has been dramatizing myths, folk tales and legends from diverse cultures for over 35 years. One of the original residents of Westbeth, Lee moved there with his family in 1970. He is currently on the faculty at NYU.

As a child growing up in Vermont, Ralph Lee discovered two passions he would pursue for the rest of his life: puppetry and the theater. "All my teenage years I made puppets and masks," he says. "I would take them around to birthday parties and schools and do shows. Theater is something I really connected with very early on as well. I was in my first play when I was seven. It was a play in our one-room schoolhouse and I played a cat. After that, I was hooked!"

After graduating from Amherst College in 1957, Lee studied dance and theater in Europe for two years on a Fulbright Scholarship. Returning stateside, he moved to New York to act and began creating masks, puppets, and larger-than-life figures for theater and dance companies. "It happened one year that I taught for a semester at Bennington College," he recalls. "They wanted me to do a production so I chose to do an 'almost-pageant' that took place outdoors and moved around the campus. The students made a lot of masks and giant puppets and I brought up stuff that I had made for other shows as well. I had never done anything like that before: the logistics, the costumes, and the large cast. It turned out to be a surprisingly successful event."

Is this how the Village Halloween Parade come about? "Theatre for the New City had been bugging me to do something for Halloween and in 1974 I finally agreed," Lee says. "Doing that event at Bennington had given me confidence so I felt able to embark on a larger project.

I can't remember who said the word 'parade' but it seemed like it was in all our minds. We envisioned it as a mile-long theatrical extravaganza snaking through the Village."

"I really liked those early days because people could enter and leave the parade at any point," Lee continues. "By the fifth year the crowds were so large we had to erect barricades and the whole feeling changed. My wish all along had been that people would come and see this parade and then go back to their own communities and start their own. But that's not what happened." After running the parade for 12 years, Lee decided to give up the reins. "I was ready to do it," he admits. "The final year that I did it was the first year it moved to Sixth Avenue. I'm definitely happy that it's still going. I wouldn't have wanted it to disappear but the feel of community was hard to sustain once the route changed. I felt it was time for me to move away and I've honestly never regretted that."

As a long-time resident of the West Village, Lee is grateful that he's had the opportunity to be here, and that Westbeth has been "a wonderful place to live." However, he does have some regrets. "It's not fun the way it used to be and much of that is financial," he says. "Due to commercial interests, a lot of people were squeezed out. As far as the people living here now, well you have to practically be a millionaire to do so. That really changes things." He laughs. "That's pretty simplistic, but it's the way it feels."

Even more indicative of change is the fact that a Halloween parade could probably never get off the ground now. "It's interesting," Lee says. "It seems to me that it would be very difficult to start an event like this nowadays. It happened at a time in the Village when things were more open and there was more sense of community. So many residents along the route would open their doors and let us set up lights in their apartments and put our 'creatures' on their rooftops and fire escapes. It really shifted the feel of the environment to be able to do that. But I can't imagine that people nowadays would open their doors that way."

In other words, the Halloween parade was the product of a different West Village. "It was a wonderful coming together of just the right elements," Lee agrees. "It's hard to imagine that happening again in the City at this point."

West Village Original • Community Activism

Joan McAllister

September 2013

Joan McAllister was born in Los Angeles in 1929. For the past 26 years McAllister has edited and published a monthly informational newsletter for families in New York City shelters named "How...When...Where." A resident of Charles Street since 1970, she still lives in her brownstone with her two West Highland terriers.

As a young woman, Joan McAllister had the firm idea that what you did after college was stay home for a year, get some kind of job, and then move to Paris. So that was just what she did after graduating from Stanford with a degree in journalism. "After a year I decided to go to Europe and took my mother," she says. "The two of us traveled for four months and had a wonderful time. But I decided I was too young to live overseas. On the way home, Mother dropped me off in New York. She left me in a hotel on 49th Street and 1st Avenue. That's where I started out and I got a job with *Newsweek*." McAllister was there for four years but left when it became clear that editorial positions went to the men on staff. "So I went to NBC instead," she says. "It was amazing! I was hired immediately as a writer in public affairs. Television was less old fashioned about women."

In 1960 McAllister married her husband, John, an editor at *Newsweek*. "I retired from being a paid writer because I wanted to raise my kids," she says. By the 1980s, with the children grown and now a widow, McAllister started casting about for something to do. "I was entertaining myself by doing a lot of volunteer work," she says. "In particular, I was very involved with the homeless crisis in New York and the shelter system that grew up around it. I discovered that there were a lot of services available to families in shelters that they didn't know about. Someone said to me that we needed a newsletter that would provide that information. So we brought out the first issue of *How...When...Where* in June of 1987." According to McAllister, it's still pretty much the same publication today. "We give advice about getting a job, receiving legal aid, or finding healthcare," she says. "We list sports activities for kids. I have one writer who's an expert on children with disabilities and I have people from Legal Services who write for me as well." And does she continue to enjoy publishing it? "Oh, yes," she admits. "I love it! I'm quite convinced the information is useful and that we came up with a good solution for getting it out there. Although I'm getting old and I'm going to have to hand the newsletter over to someone else soon!"

A resident of the City since 1952, McAllister and her husband moved to Charles Street in 1970. "It was probably the last time anybody but a millionaire could purchase a house around here," she says. But when asked how much the West Village has changed since moving here, McAllister not only doesn't have a list of complaints, she has to admit she doesn't see much change. "It's terrible, but when anyone starts talking about change, I have to admit I don't see any at all," she confesses. "It feels like the same place to me. I can't tell the difference like everybody else seems to. You assume if someone buys a house here nowadays they must be wealthy, but they just look like Villagers to me. And it's the same atmosphere as it's always been."

"Right now I'm standing at my window looking out on Charles Street and it looks like it did 40 years ago," she continues. "The fact that we can't change the outsides of our buildings contributes to this feeling that nothing's any different. The restaurants all look like the same kinds of restaurants. People dress pretty much like they've always dressed. I've been going to the same deli every morning for decades. So if there have been changes, I'm clearly missing some clues!"

All this adds up to one very satisfied longtime West Village resident. "I can't imagine living in any other part of town," she says. "I'm sure that shows a certain lack of imagination but I think it's a wonderful place to live. It's got everything I need. I also thought it was a wonderful place to raise my kids." McAllister stops to think a second. "Although, perhaps I should ask them," she says, laughing. "They're both living in completely different environments now! But I picked a place that was completely different from what I grew up in myself. We all do that."

West Village Original • Community Activism

Keith Michael

August 2013

Pennsylvania-born Keith Michael is the author of WestView's monthly bird column. He leads the NYC WILD! nature walks and recently published "Once Around the Block: A Birder's Year in the West Village". Michael has been Dance Production Coordinator of the Juilliard School for 17 years and lives with his partner, David, and their dog, Millie, on Perry Street.

Photo: Maggie Berkvist

While still in elementary school, Keith Michael started his own marionette company, continuing through high school and eventually paying for his first year of college with proceeds from his shows. Of course, having supportive parents helped. "My folks were thrilled by my marionette work," he says. "My mother was my stagehand and drove me to gigs before I could drive myself. I also studied piano and French horn, so classical music was another area of interest."

Thanks to his marionette work, Michael became interested in theatre and attended Case Western Reserve to pursue it. "But I ended up studying a lot of dance instead," he says. "When I graduated in 1979, I came to New York and got dancing work right away." From there he began choreographing and then, seventeen years ago, he began his association with The Juilliard School. "I started there at an age—as dancers do—when you begin looking for the next thing," he says. "It was my organizing skills that got me the job. It turned out that all of the things I had done since I was young enabled me to see things from lots of different points of view and to coordinate very big, complicated shows."

And how did his interest in birding begin? "It started out as just a hobby," Michael says. "It was something very different from my work. Everything I do is about organizing and scheduling and I was really in need of something less structured that would get me outside."

He considers birding to be a logical extension of his early fascination with the City, ever since his family came here in 1964 to visit the World's Fair. "That trip was a real eye opener for me," he remembers. "I realized there are fantastic things out there. Since then I've been very interested in New York. It's fascinating both geographically and historically. For me, birding became a natural way for me to further explore and discover it."

According to Michael, birding makes going out of his apartment exciting every day. "There's the excitement of what you're going to see," he says. "That's what I love about it." In addition, he tries to imagine the bird's perspective. "What does all this look like to a little bit of feathers?" he wonders. "Often migrating birds lead very dangerous and complicated lives. They summer here but winter in, say, Peru. So this little thing that you could mail in a first class envelope is able to fly thousands of miles and survive. And then end up in the West Village and raise a family! How do they do that? That's the captivating thing about them." To date, Michael posits that the number of bird species he's spotted in the city is around 300. Just in the West Village alone he's seen around 84.

After living in various neighborhoods throughout the City, Michael settled in the West Village in 1991. "Certainly over that long a period of time, everything changes," he observes. "But I do miss some of the businesses that can no longer afford to be here. I think the very thing that attracts people to live here—the neighborhood services—is disappearing because of the influx of money. Having unlimited money means that you don't need as many neighborhood services, like the Laundromat or the hardware store. Local services become less important if you can afford to go anywhere for them."

"You'd also like to be sure the reasons people want to live here don't disappear," he continues. "People come here for the quaintness and the cozy streets, but it's no longer cozy if apartment buildings keep going up and there are too many people." Still, Michael loves living here. "It's always fascinating," he says. "I love walking out my door and seeing such interesting architecture, people, birds, and dogs. When I was growing up we lived in little towns throughout Pennsylvania that had fewer people than live on Perry Street. But the West Village is actually much more small town than most small towns are nowadays. You have everything you need within a block or two of your front door. It's a great place to live."

West Village Original • Community Activism

Ethel Paley
January 2011

Ethel Paley has lived in the West Village since 1949. Ms. Paley was honored as a 2010 L'Oreal "Woman of Worth" for her decades-long association with FRIA, an organization dedicated to making sure that seniors get proper care, services, and treatment from nursing homes in New York State. Ms. Paley was FRIA's first executive director and still serves on the Board.

"I was born in Flushing in 1920," says Ethel Paley. "There were still a lot of farms in Queens at that point. My family moved to Connecticut during the Depression and then I came back and have lived in New York since the end of World War II. I'm glad to be able to say I'm both alive and very well."

Paley spent the war years in Washington, D.C., having the experience of a lifetime. "I served in the WAVES," Paley remembers. "I took on the kind of desk jobs that the men who were in active duty used to have. Let me say any experience like that opens you up to ideas and to people that you might not have ordinarily met. I came from a very small town in Connecticut and while my parents were pretty sophisticated, my own experience was much more limited. Some of the people I met and the ideas that I encountered in the service had a big influence on me. It was a great experience and Washington, of course, was a *very* interesting place at that time."

After her service, Paley returned to finish her education, ending up with a degree in Social Work from Columbia. It was this career path that eventually led her to Friends and Relatives of Institutionalized Aged (FRIA). "I had been working on geriatric programs when I was hired by them," she recalls. "FRIA was organized right after the nursing home scandals of the mid-1970s, when it was clear how difficult it was for even very well-educated families to understand how the nursing home system worked. Our task was to both guide and safeguard our client's loved ones who were in these facilities. To this day, we don't suggest solutions but we talk about what options are available in any kind of circumstance. And even though it was descriptive, our full name still reeked of a 'social work' look at the world, so we eventually dropped it and just use FRIA instead."

"Personally, it's been enormously satisfying," Paley says of her experience with FRIA. "I feel every time I'm in the office or out in the field, I'm learning something new. We've had our wins and we've also been frustrated by what we couldn't accomplish. But most of those frustrations have been financial." Sadly, the current recession has pushed FRIA to the brink due to the difficulty of raising funds. "While I think the need for our services is still very real, we might have to suspend operations," Paley laments. "This is very hard news to convey to anyone. We're not giving up our non-profit status, but we're going to have to look for new approaches and new funding."

As a longtime resident of the West Village, Paley mentions one spot where the change has been most dramatic. "I would say both Eighth Street and Sixth Avenue have become so tacky," she says. "Eighth Street used to be a Mom and Pop type neighborhood; a genuine small town Main Street with good delis, restaurants, and small stores of all types. This changed for the worse over the years. My own neighborhood has been changed in recent years by the proliferations of designer stores on Bleecker Street. Instead of being tacky, they're just glitzy in their own right. And also nothing that most of us can afford! I do none of my shopping here now but in my time you could be very self-sufficient and almost never leave the West Village."

After six decades here, though, it's not hard for Paley to express her love for the West Village. "It's still the best place in New York City and probably the second-best place to live in the whole wide world," she says. What's first? "In my view that would be Paris," she admits, laughing. "But the Village is really very special. I think there are those of us who might not be happy with the changes over the years, but neighborhoods have to evolve. Actually, my two daughters are feeling that it's become so much more of a yuppie community than it used to be. But it's home to me, and I feel comfortable here. I'm happy to still be able to visit the establishments that I've known over the years and welcome many of the new ones."

West Village Original • Community Activism

Allen Pilikian

May 2013

Allen Pilikian is currently the Vice Chairman of Jefferson Market Garden. Born in Lenox Hill Hospital and raised in Manhattan and on Long Island, he has been associated with the garden since its inception 38 years ago. A former fiscal director for the city's Human Resources Administration, Pilikian currently lives in Douglas Manor, Queens.

"I was always very interested in nature and ornithology, ever since I was a kid," Allen Pilikian says. "I loved to go hiking in the woods with friends and go bird watching. I just loved flowers and trees and I knew a lot about them. My grandparents also had gardens at their various homes." It was this love of gardens that would lead Pilikian to help create an urban version of one with the beautiful Jefferson Market Garden. However, there was a lot of work to be done first.

When Pilikian moved to West 9th Street in 1972, the Village was struggling. "There was a great deal of street crime and an enormous amount of vandalism, particularly of cars," he recalls. "I can remember having to walk over shattered glass on the sidewalk two or three days a week. Another issue was garbage all over the place: on the sidewalks, in the street, it was a pigsty." Then there was the 13-story Women's House of Detention, a WPA project built right next to the Jefferson Market Court House and later the Library. "It was a dreadful eyesore," Pilikian says. "Most of the poor women who were incarcerated there were prostitutes with drug problems. Their pimps would come down and stand on the sidewalk and have arguments with them. Things would be thrown out of windows and a symphony of foul language would be screamed back and forth. The local residents hated that."

In response to these quality of life issues, that period saw a proliferation of block associations and advocacy groups. Pilikian joined The Greenwich Village Committee for the Jefferson Market Area, incorporated as a nonprofit 501(c)3. It raised money and pressured city, state, and federal officials to demolish the prison. "At every level, they were all in support of our efforts," Pilikian says. "They got a bill out of the City Council and a demolition contract was overwhelmingly approved to tear down the prison. Mayor Lindsay signed it, the ladies were moved to Rikers Island, scaffolding went up, and the prison came down."

The next step was actually creating a garden on the plot. "That was not a very easy thing to do," Pilikian remembers. "What really started the ball rolling was when Mrs. Astor came and viewed the property. A few weeks later the Astor Fund gave us $33,000, which was a lot of money back then, particularly for a pile of dirt! That gave our organization a lot of street credibility and other grants came in. Later on, Mrs. Astor gave us another $250,000 to recreate the original fence around the garden."

Years later, when Pilikian took over as Vice Chairman of the garden it was still closed to the public. "Considering the time it started, that made sense," he says. "But this was quite a number of years later and a lot of the criminal element was gone. I felt the garden was a great Village resource and that its viability depended upon linking it primarily to those who lived here. So I asked the board to open up the garden to the public." What was their response? "They went nuts," he responds, laughing. "They said they wouldn't approve it, citing such things as 'homeless people' and 'garbage.' So we compromised. I bought two benches to put in the garden as an experiment. People came in by the droves. Now we have eight benches and people love the garden!"

Pilikian no longer lives in the Village, but between his garden duties and visiting friends, he still spends a lot of time in here. "It's become a much more beautiful place," he observes. "Much more green with trees and plantings, much safer, and much cleaner. It's improved vastly in every way." Does he miss living here? "I definitely do," he says. "But I consider myself very fortunate to have lived there all those years. Starting when I was a teenager and I would go down there with friends. Not to raise Cain or do anything illegal, but just to look at the architecture, to explore, to go to the cafés for a cup of coffee, and to people watch. Because let's face it, you still get a lot of interesting characters walking around Greenwich Village!"

West Village Original • Community Activism

David Rothenberg

February 2010

David Rothenberg has lived in the city since 1959 and in the West Village since 1964. While producing an Off-Broadway play about prison in 1967, he founded The Fortune Society, which supports successful re-entry into society for formerly incarcerated men and women. Today the Society boasts over 175 full- and part-time employees. David also does a radio show on WBAI every Saturday morning.

For David Rothenberg, born in 1933 across the river in Hackensack, the West Village was always the place he was destined to be.

"My family used to tell me that when I was four or five and they first brought me into the city I looked around and said, 'Thank God there's something else!'" he relays, laughing. "I always knew the Village was where I wanted to live. However, when I got out of the Army I first took an apartment uptown. I had a series of jobs and then began to work for a theatrical press agent. Producer Alexander Cohn hired me to handle the press for all of his shows. One of them was Richard Burton's *Hamlet*. This was while he was having his very public affair with Elizabeth Taylor so it was an exciting time! After that, I needed a vacation so I took a freighter to Italy where I became enamored of their piazzas. When I returned I found an apartment on Sheridan Square, calling it 'my piazza'. That was 1964 and I've been in the West Village ever since."

How did a theatrical press agent start something like The Fortune Society? "In 1967 I produced a play called *Fortune and Men's Eyes* at the Actors Playhouse," Rothenberg recalls. "It was a gritty play about what happens to a kid who goes to prison, written by a man who had been there himself. I used my life savings—$12,000 at the time—to produce it because no one else would. It was a success, and we started a dialogue with the audience after the performances. Joining us on stage were people who had been in prison and I was moved by their struggles to re-enter society. I said, 'We should start educating the public about the kinds of job and housing barriers you're all facing.' So my theater office on 46th Street became the headquarters for the Society. By 1971 I had to make a career choice so I gave up theatre and for the next 18 years I was full-time director of the Society. After I ran for City Council in 1985 and lost, I went back to the theater and re-opened my press office. I retired from that in 2001, but I'm still more heavily involved with the Fortune Society than I ever was."

When asked what the Village was like when he first moved here, Rothenberg responds, "Wonderful! It was where I wanted to be, the part of the universe that attracted me. Off-Broadway theatre started here in the Village. Everything was free, non-judgmental, and creative. The Bagel and the Riviera were hangouts. There were always the jazz clubs like the Village Gate. You could go to Bigelow's late at night and get a sandwich or an early breakfast at three or four in the morning."

Yet Rothenberg doesn't dwell on the past for too long, particularly since some things have improved. "I love what they've done down by the piers," he says. "It's nicer than it ever was. And opening the Center on 13th Street so that gay people have a place to go was exciting." He does worry, though, about sky-high housing prices putting pressure on preservation efforts. "It's always about the real estate people," he says ruefully. "They've become the oil tycoons of Manhattan! Jane Jacobs always said, 'Save the neighborhoods. That's what makes a city strong.' The Village is a wonderful neighborhood and it should be preserved."

Does he have any final thoughts on being a resident of the West Village? "Just about how lucky I am to be here for all these years," Rothenberg readily admits. "When I first got here all you heard was 'Everything was great twenty or thirty years ago!' I'm very nostalgic myself about the days when I came here. I look back and I miss things. You soon realize, though, that what you're really missing is your youth, when it was all new and fresh. But I'm not one of those people who think that everything great happened in the past. I still feel this neighborhood is exciting. That's because people who march to a different drummer come to the Village. They always will."

West Village Original • Community Activism

Arthur Z. Schwartz
March 2009

Arthur Z. Schwartz settled in the West Village in 1981. Currently a lawyer and partner in a Union-side labor and employment firm, he was also just hired as general counsel for ACORN. Beginning in 1995, Schwartz was elected to five consecutive terms as the Democratic Party District Leader for Greenwich Village and South Chelsea. In 2006 he was elected New York State Democratic Committee Member for the 66th Assembly District.

"I love the West Village, but I think I picked it by accident," confesses Arthur Z. Schwartz. For the Bronx-born attorney, it wasn't the first neighborhood he had in mind. "In 1981, I actually bought a little building on 6th Street in the East Village," he recalls. "My mother was giving me the money for it so I asked her to come to the signing. She looked at the building and afterward, at dinner, started to cry, saying, 'I don't want you to live on a block like this!' So I canceled the contract and decided I wanted to live in the West Village instead. I walked around the entire neighborhood until one day I noticed an apartment for rent at 99 Bank Street. Here I still am 28 years later."

It was also Schwartz's mother from whom he got his sense of community service. "She had a penchant for volunteering for many different causes," he remembers. "She wasn't political, though. She was more interested in activism on the local level." Taking it one step further, Schwartz parlayed his community service into political office. In 1990 he founded Friends of Bleecker Playground and went on to hold such various positions as member of the Executive Committee of Village Independent Democrats; member of Community Board 2 in Manhattan; park activist for the West Village; and Board member, Hudson River Park Alliance and Friends of Hudson River Park. It was this last position that got him elected to his first term as Democratic District Leader.

For Schwartz, this maiden voyage into elected office came at a price because it cost him a lot of support. "Most West Villagers were against the Hudson River Park. They thought it was about luxury housing and massive development," he explains. "I first bought into that as well. Then when I got elected in 1995 I began seeing it as a potential recreational place and I became a leader in the effort to build it. I lost a lot of friends who accused me of selling out. I think most of those people got over it, but it took a long time." For Schwartz, this support for unpopular issues is par for the course. "I'm not someone who worries about going against the tide," he admits. "I've learned to grit my teeth and deal with being a contrarian if I think it's the right thing to do."

When asked how the West Village has changed since he first moved here, Schwartz mentions three things. "First, I would say that the Village was much more economically diverse," he says. "There were a few co-ops but most people who lived here were tenants in rent-stabilized or rent-controlled apartments. They were mostly struggling artists of some sort, an amazing array of them. Secondly, it's become much more family-friendly. That's a big change. And third is that the West Village was much more gay. Today it hardly is. A lot of my gay neighbors died in the 80s or moved on to other areas, like Chelsea. However, I built pretty close ties with gay and lesbian activists here and that was a part of my political identity. But that's aspect has definitely changed."

As a longtime West Village resident and politician, Schwartz also has a few ideas about how he'd like to see this neighborhood in the future. "For one, I'd like to preserve the last vestiges we have of local businesses," he ventures. "Every time one of them closes I feel like a piece of us is taken away. Also, I think we've got enough high-end wealthy people. We need to maintain some economic diversity in the West Village. And I say that as a building owner who's paying $65,000 a year in property taxes! I understand the pressures on landlords. Most of my fellow non-billionaire neighbors pay huge real estate tax bills and they're struggling to stay in their houses."

Despite the challenges, living here never grows old for Schwartz. "There's a special quality to the West Village," he declares. "It's amazing how many people you know when you walk down the street. It's like a small town. I find it incredible to live in New York in a low-rise neighborhood that's close knit and friendly and yet be fifteen minutes from Times Square. I can't imagine ever leaving."

West Village Original • Community Activism

Whitney North Seymour, Jr.

November 2008

Born in 1923 and a lifelong New Yorker, attorney Whitney North Seymour served in the New York State senate from 1966–68. He was also U.S. attorney for the Southern District of New York from 1970–73 when he represented the government in its fight to prevent the New York Times from publishing the Pentagon Papers.

"For me, the West Village has always been characterized by action and involvement," says Whitney North Seymour, Jr. "And three kinds of action at that: individual, community, and political." A resident of West 11th Street since he and his wife, Catryna, moved there as newlyweds in 1951, North has spent most of the ensuing years practicing what he preaches. For him, activism is not only a calling, but also a way to give back to what he considers a very special part of this city. "If we're going to enjoy the West Village, it's our obligation to pay it back for that privilege. You do that by giving time to local organizations and fighting against people who would exploit and ruin it."

On an individual level, one story in particular illustrates Seymour's style. "After a trip to Paris and seeing how sidewalk cafes added such life to that city," he recounts, "Catryna and I returned to New York and realized there were virtually no sidewalk cafes here. So we drove up and down the streets of the Village, writing down the addresses of bars and restaurants that were likely sites for sidewalk cafes. Then we mailed memos to the owners suggesting they put out cafes and that it would only cost—in those days—$25 for the license. Next spring there were dozens of sidewalk cafes around the village!"

The second type of action comes from the community, as Seymour explains it. There are block associations in every segment of the West Village. "They come and go as people live there and move on," he says. "But it's part of the quality of our community that I think sets it especially apart, including some of the bigger groups like the Greenwich Village Society for Historical Preservation. Within my time, Jane Jacobs was very active and vocal in espousing the notion of what makes cities great in terms of participation and scale."

As for political action, it was by running for elected offices that Seymour learned some valuable lessons. "The village was a wonderful hotbed of political reform in the 50s and 60s. At that time, I was Assistant DA and was urged by others to get involved in the political process on the proposition that everyone complains about politics but no one does anything about it." Amazingly enough, all three of his appointed positions came after he ran for public office and was defeated. "That was because I had shown my willingness to fight," he remembers. "As a result, I came to people's attention."

For Seymour, the overriding benefit of being a politician was what it teaches you about human relations. "Working in politics teaches you respect for different people," he says. "In politics, you learn that even though others don't have the same background as you, good people still try to do what they believe is the right thing. That's an experience that shapes you for life. I believe the highest responsibility for a human being is to show respect for other people. And I mean on the ground; showing kindness to those who need a helping hand or are lost. The political process is part of what makes you learn how to do that."

When asked what's the biggest change he's seen in the West Village, he quickly responds, "Gentrification. It's not as scruffy as it used to be. Not scruffy in a derogatory sense but in the sense that people were more natural. You saw and felt the bubbling excitement of people who were doing creative work, having meetings, protesting wrong policies of the government, fighting Robert Moses, or saving the Jefferson Market courthouse. You don't see much of that anymore. "

It's not all bad, however. "The undercurrent is still there," Seymour admits. "You still find people who want to support creative ideas. You see young people hoping to write their first novel or their first play or paint their first masterpiece. You see people sketching on the street corner. And last night on our block there was a fellow sitting on a chair and playing a cello. It was wonderful."

> "
> I actually find the Village more exciting and interesting than in the old days, when it was just rough. We've also become very polite. We didn't used to be that way when we didn't have tourists in the neighborhood. Now it's full of them.
> "
>
> —Vincent Livelli

Jackson Square Park

West Village Original • Culinary Arts

Suzy Chase

April 2019

Cookbook podcaster Suzy Chase was born in Illinois in 1967 and raised in Prairie Village, Kansas. Her podcast, "Cookery by the Book," airs from her dining room table. She also recently wrapped up a six-year happy hour DJ residency at Trophy Bar in Williamsburg. A neighborhood resident for 23 years, Chase lives on West 4th Street with her husband, Bob, and son, JP.

As a girl growing up in the Midwest, Suzy Chase would lie in bed at night, trying to tune into distant stations on her radio. "I've always loved radio," she says. "My parents, who were both born in 1929, grew up with radio so as a child when I said, 'I can't sleep,' my Mom would say 'Turn on your radio!' If the weather was good, I could get WLA in Chicago, which was a biggie, or WCCO out of Minneapolis. Even back when I was a kid I loved Sally Jesse Raphael. Larry King was so good on the radio! Art Bell was another one I listened to. I love the intimacy of conversation over the radio and simply listening to two people talking."

After high school, Chase went on to study at the University at Kansas in Lawrence. "It's a really good journalism school," she says. "I studied broadcasting there. In fact, after my sophomore year I got a job offer while I was interning at a radio station in Kansas City. My Mom let me quit college and take the job."

How did the marriage between podcasting and cooking come about? "I was doing radio in the evenings in Kansas City," Chase says. "I wanted a daytime job as well, so I started doing publicity for a cookbook publishing company. That's where I got the background. I'm not innately a great cook and that's why I like a good recipe that I can follow. I love reading cookbooks and recipes and discovering the stories behind them. It's always interesting to me why the author wrote them."

Chase does her podcast from her dining room table via audio Skype. "Since 2015, it's been the only podcast devoted to cookbooks," she says. "I interview the author after I've cooked a recipe out of their book. I do the cooking in my tiny kitchen and then we talk about it, discussing not only ingredients and my success or failure with the recipe, but about them as well. I feel like I get a lot of information about an author when I cook one of their recipes. I think that every cookbook has a story." According to Chase, response has been great. "I get approximately 7,000 downloads per episode and I have over 10,000 subscribers to the RSS feed. Food is so hot now. Everyone's into food!"

What brought Chase to the West Village? "I just always had this thing about New York City," she says. "One day in 1995 I looked up and thought if I don't get out of Kansas City now, I never will. I always loved watching the intro to *Saturday Night Live* where they show images of the City. I was like, 'Everyone's up and doing things. And here they're all asleep!' On a whim, I started looking for jobs here and I found one doing publicity for a publisher. I kind of crowbarred my way into it. I asked them why didn't they start a cookbook division and they said I could do that when I got here!"

"When I arrived, my broker showed me apartments in different parts of the City," she continues. "Then he showed me something on Perry Street. I didn't know where I was, but it just hit me. 'This is it! I love it!' It just felt right. And you know what I did? I asked him if it was a safe neighborhood!" She laughs. "I just went with my gut and my gut was right on. It's homey here. People are nice and super interesting." Has it changed much? "Oh, my gosh, yes," Chase responds. "Since I moved here in 1996, so many families have moved in. It used to be single haven. Even twelve years ago when I was pregnant I didn't see many other pregnant gals here. That's definitely changed!"

What hasn't changed is Chase's fondness for this part of town or her delight in being here. "Who needs to go above 14th Street? That's what I say," she says, laughing. "My podcast is very West Village-centric. I'm always talking about how I cook in my tiny West Village kitchen and I include numerous West Village photos on my Instagram page. It's sort of my unique love letter to this neighborhood."

West Village Original • Culinary Arts

Anita Lo

December 2019

Chef and cookbook author Anita Lo was born in Detroit in 1965. From 2000–17, Lo owned the Michelin-starred restaurant Annisa on Barrow Street. She has appeared on Top Chef Masters, Iron Chef America, and Chopped. In 2015 she became the first female guest chef to cook at the White House. She is the author of the cookbook "Solo."

When chef Anita Lo moved to New York City to attend Columbia University, it was to major in French literature. "But what are you going to do with a degree in that?" she asks, laughing. "When I continued my French studies at Columbia's campus in Paris I fell in love with the country. French culture is very food-focused as well, so I ended up taking some cooking classes at a place called La Varenne. And this time I also fell in love with cooking. I did finish my degree but when I returned to New York I went to work in several restaurants, including Chanterelle and Bouley."

"Cooking provides a sort of semi-immediate satisfaction and I've always liked to work with my hands," she continues. "I think the life style suited me as well because I've never been a morning person. Lastly, I was not a very gender-conforming youth so going into corporate America wouldn't have been a good fit for me. No way." As for a particular cuisine, she claims to like it all. "My restaurant Annisa was contemporary American," Lo says. "And as befits this vast country we live in it was a multi-cultural cuisine. But my technique is French and upon that I can build flavors from all over the world."

In 2000, Lo and her business partner opened Annisa on Barrow Street. What did she like best about owning a restaurant? "Following my dream and working with food," Lo says. "Making people happy was one of the good parts. It was a privilege to come up with a dish that I was proud of and have people appreciate it. And being able to have a team that worked so well together. After we had the fire in 2009, the restaurant was closed for nine months. People always ask me what my crowning career moment was, thinking I might say cooking for 250 people at the Obama White House. But for me it was when we reopened the restaurant. My entire staff came back with me. It was kind of amazing."

Would Lo ever open another restaurant? "No, not at all," she replies. "I've done it. Real estate has gotten ridiculous in the West Village and taxes went way up for me. In addition, no cook can actually afford to live here, so it's become difficult to hire staff. There's nothing more stressful than that. Our concept for Annisa was less expensive fine dining and we couldn't make that affordable anymore. We were getting squeezed from all sides and I was burnt out."

Since closing the restaurant Lo has been busy, not least with the publication of her cookbook *Solo*, a play on both her last name and cooking for one. "I was talking with a friend about cookbook titles and 'solo' came up. I thought, 'I have to write that!' It could be easy and funny, and we could poke fun at how people see eating alone. The reaction to the book has been great." In addition, Lo has been running culinary tours both nationally and internationally. "I work with an outfit called Tour de Forks. The groups are small, and I usually teach a cooking class at the end of it. The class is about my take on the cuisine of the country we happen to be in."

Lo bought her walk-up apartment on Barrow Street at the bottom of the market in the 90s. After a recent knee replacement made it difficult to climb stairs, she looked into getting another place around here. "Well, prices have exploded, and it didn't take me long to realize, 'Nope, my apartment is going to be just fine for the rest of my life!'" she says, laughing. "Luckily, I do feel like it's the best neighborhood to be in. It is a village. I know everyone who lives here. And it's also a great restaurant neighborhood, so for me it's about discovery and to see what other people are doing in their kitchens. As a cook, I'm definitely inspired by others. I love eating at home, but there's nothing better than eating out. I don't think I could ever have owned a restaurant if I didn't like eating out."

West Village Original • Dance

Vincent Livelli

July 2018

Vincent Livelli was born in Brooklyn in 1920, baptized at St. Anthony's on Sullivan Street, and raised in Greenwich Village. A former professional dancer, he held jobs as cruise director on ships for over 20 years. Despite being hearing impaired since he was a child, Livelli also learned five languages which, not surprisingly, he claims was a great asset during his career. He lives on Perry Street.

As a child growing up in Greenwich Village, Vincent Livelli had to overcome a hearing impairment that neither his family nor teachers were equipped to handle. So he learned to be resourceful. "At night I would put the radio under my pillow and was able to absorb the music while lying down in bed," he says. "My father would say, 'Shut that that damn thing off. I'm trying to go to sleep!,' but I was married to the radio. Because of my impairment, it was easier for me to absorb drumbeats and that's why I was drawn to Cuban music. I felt touched by the drums. I would call it 'divine music': music from outer space. That's because sound waves never die. Light waves diminish, but sound waves have been known by scientists to exist forever."

This early exposure to Cuban rhythm and music would lead Livelli—as a young man in the late 1930s—to a Cuban dance hall called the Park Plaza in East Harlem where the house orchestra was called The Happy Boys. "I would go and hang out there," he says. "They thought I was a cop because I was taller than anyone else! One night they asked me why I didn't dance and I replied that I didn't know how. I couldn't even dance the Fox Trot back then. So a heavy woman named Estella took me out on the floor and that was the first step I took into the world of dancing. I went on to teach Latin dancing—bolero, merengue, tango, rumba—all over Miami in the 1940s. I had ended up there from attending the University of Miami. It was easy to find work because all the hotels had to have a Latin dance team. Everybody wanted to learn it. From there it was just a step to teaching dance on cruise ships and eventually I graduated to cruise director."

What was it about the life of cruising on ships that appealed to Livelli? "I like to say that it's 'yoga afloat'," he replies. "When you're on a ship you're calmly moving in a way you don't normally do. While the feeling on land is hurly-burly, on the sea it's extraordinarily calm. You're also eating beautiful food and you're surrounded by pure air. If you can stand the boredom, it's a wonderful life!" He laughs. "I stood it because the job provided me with comfort, money, food, commissions from merchants, and romance, which meant dancing under the stars. That sort of life is exquisite. I also felt I was there to make people happy because without happiness what is life?"

By the time he retired, Livelli had sailed on 64 ships, been around the world, and visited 60 countries. "I went on the untrodden path before there was one!" he says. "The ships started to grow in size and amenities, too. My first ship—the *SS Dominicano*, which did winter cruises out of Miami—wasn't even air-conditioned. At the end of my career ships were many times bigger and offered all sorts of entertainment, much of it thanks to me. I think I had a beautiful life and that's why I'm able to boast a little. Travel makes you happier than anything else that I know."

Livelli wonders if he's "not a true Villager" because he left for many years after high school, living abroad or on ships instead. But since settling back down here, he's changed his mind. "It's where my heart is," he admits. "I actually find the Village more exciting and interesting than in the old days, when it was just rough. Now we have all these well-dressed actors, models and show business people living along these expensive streets. We've also become very polite. We didn't used to be that way when we didn't have tourists in the neighborhood. Now it's full of them. You say 'Greenwich Village' anywhere in the world these days and people know of it."

West Village Original • Dance

Edith Stephen
March 2017

Dancer and filmmaker Edith Stephen was born in Salamanca, New York, in 1919 and grew up in Brooklyn. For years she toured the U.S., Europe, and China with her dance troupe until taking up film-making. One of the original tenants of Westbeth, Stephen's fifth and latest documentary is "The Invisible Writer Who Becomes Visible." She is also featured in the film "Winter in Westbeth," a celebration of creativity in the elderly.

Although she was born into a strict, Orthodox Jewish family, Edith Stephen's parents were determined she and her sister grow up to be Americans first. "My parents had emigrated here and had an arranged marriage as well," she says. "But they were also individuals. They let us do whatever we wanted so that we would be Americans in America. They didn't want us to be Russian or Polish like them. But I was always very happy that I had that background as well. It made me appreciate people who are different from me."

This freedom allowed Stephen to take a less conventional path through life. "I didn't follow the normal way of going about things," she says. "But when it came to dancing, I was a natural. I always say that I jumped out of my mother's belly dancing. Actually, though, when I started to dance people told me, 'Oh, you're too old to dance.' I was 15 when they said that! But I stuck to it, became a choreographer and started my own company. And I traveled the world doing it. That sounds big, doesn't it? 'The world!'" She laughs.

"I think everybody should dance," she continues. "I always claim I got to this age because I was a dancer. Doctors and researchers now say that the immune system can cure cancer but I could have told them that! Dancing is great for the immune system because it's the one thing that involves every part of you if you're doing the right kind. It's immensely exciting, too, because it's about you and your body does not lie. When a person walks into a room, right away you get something from them—either good or bad—by the way they move. I could sit here and know a person a block away just by the way they walk."

After Stephen hung up her dancing shoes, she turned to making films. She claims the transition was made easier by the fact that from the start, her dances always told a story and she used mixed media to tell it. "I had poetry in my dance," she says. "I had film, sculpture, and painting as well. Of course dance was the important thing. So it was very easy for me to transfer to film because it has all those same elements in it. It was just a different medium. But I tell you that I could never do film if it wasn't for video. It's made it so easy."

When Stephen married her husband in 1942, they first lived in Brooklyn. Later they moved to various apartments in the Village until Westbeth opened, becoming some of its very first tenants. "I think that the Village is one of the really exciting places in the City," she says. "But when our last mayor, Michael Bloomberg, transformed this place into Millionaires Row I felt like I lost both my Bohemian life and my home." And, closer to home, changes are palpable as well, if for other reasons. "These days, if you open my apartment door the public spaces are empty," she says. "But 20 years ago Westbeth was rocking with people in the hallways! They were talking, or fighting, or bringing food to each other. It was a real community. Today there's not one person in the entire hallway. There's no communication anymore except through your fingers. It's a different world."

Stephen will turn 98 years old on April 2nd. Does she have any thoughts on such an accomplishment? "I don't consider turning 98 an accomplishment," she says. "Instead, I think that everybody should grow young as they grow old. They should be active. Life is living! Too many people are defeated by the idea that they're old, so they become old. I always believed I was young. I watch little children and they're so adventurous and curious and that's what we lose as we grow older. Never lose your curiosity!"

West Village Original • Dance

Vija Vetra

June 2011

Photo: Vija Vetra, London, 1962

Dancer Vija Vetra was born in Riga, Latvia in 1923 and has been a WestBeth resident since 1970. Ms. Vetra has travelled the world as a solo dancer specializing in various styles, from modern to Indian. Since 1990, she has returned every year to her native country to teach master classes at the national theatre, receiving from the government the Award of Three Stars, their highest civilian honor.

When Vija Vetra was growing up in her native Riga, music and dance were inextricably woven together. "Since I can remember, whenever I heard music I reacted to it with dance and movement. Music is very potent in my life and I always liked to move to it. The first instrument I danced to was the guitar because my father played it."

It was after seeing a local production of Swan Lake that she decided she wanted to study dance professionally. But her family was against it. "So I ran away to Vienna to live with my aunt," she says. "I was 16. She also didn't want me to become a dancer, so I had everyone against me. I knew what I wanted, though. I knew it was my destiny. You either know it or you don't." Vetra did indeed find the opportunity to study dance in Vienna. However, World War II began and the intervening years were a struggle for her and her family.

When the war ended, Vetra immigrated to Australia with her sister, mother, and aunt. She lived there for 16 years, opening her own studio, starting her own dance group, and having her own television program. "I was very well-known in Australia," she recalls. In 1964 she was invited for a coast-to-coast dance tour of America and Canada. "I danced in 36 cities," she says. "Then I was asked to be on the faculty at Carnegie Hall so I never returned to Australia. I opened my first studio in New York on Sixth Avenue and my second in Westbeth in 1970, where I still live."

What does it feel like for her to dance? "It's very special," Vetra says. "It's a feeling of not being the everyday person that I am, but that I connect with something higher above me. The best way to put it is I am not a pedestrian anymore, but I grow wings and I fly." She feels strongly that dance has a healing power as well. "Any art form can be therapy," she says. "But dance has healing power not only for the one who dances but also for the one who looks at it. That, too, is very important. And I'm not talking about much of what happens now in dance, which is deranged art. That does not heal!" she says emphatically. "But a certain way of dance, a certain way of art which uplifts you, that heals. There's a big difference!"

As a resident of the West Village for over four decades, Vetra misses the "intimate" nature of what the Village used to be. "Bleecker Street has changed so much," she laments. "It had these nice little boutiques, very nice restaurants, and mom and pop shops. Now it's become so commercial, with high fashion boutiques that can be found anywhere." However, she feels it remains the place to be if you live in New York. "I still love the Village much more than I do New York proper. When I go to midtown, I don't feel like I'm home. But once I get off a bus in the Village, I do. It's the best neighborhood in New York."

Vetra is particularly delighted with Hudson River Park. "It's a wonderful place now," she says enthusiastically. "I remember when it was those terrible wharfs. We went there on Sundays anyway, but it was very dangerous. Now what they've done on the riverside is fantastic! I really feel like I'm on the Riviera when I go there. It's a great gift to the Village."

The garden in St. Luke's is also one of her favorite spots to relax and meditate. And, finally, there are her trees. "I love all those blooming white trees on our streets in spring," she says. "I have a favorite one on Tenth Street and when I stand under it, I ask it to bless me. It's wonderful to have so many trees in the Village. I borrow strength from them. In fact, the river, St. Luke's, and my blooming trees are the places where I get in touch not only with nature but also with myself. After all, I'm part of nature as well, am I not?"

The Whitney Musem of Art

❝

*Life can be difficult at times,
but I think you're more prepared
for it if you've been fortunate
enough to grow up in a
neighborhood like this.*

❞

—Joe Lisi

West Village Original • Film & Television

Page Johnson
March 2012

Stage, film, and TV actor Page Johnson was born in West Virginia in 1922, where he made his tap-dancing debut in the local movie theatre at age 12. He has appeared with Olivia DeHaviland, Richard Burton, Anthony Perkins, Jason Robards, and Coleen Dewhurst, among others. A resident of Grove Street since 1950, Johnson can still be seen riding his bicycle around the West Village.

Growing up in a small, coal-mining town in West Virginia, Page Johnson always longed to escape. "My father got a job in a town called Welch and started a family," Johnson recalls. "My mother hated it because she was a very beautiful woman as well as an upscale lady. She ran off with a charming salesman from St. Louis when I was six. I never saw her again. It was like an Ida Lupino movie! I don't blame her, though. She hated the coalmines and she wanted to get out. Just like me. When I was three I said I wanted to get out of that town and thanks to my family's encouragement, I eventually did."

Johnson attended Ithaca College in New York in 1940, where he studied drama. "We only had money enough for a year's tuition, which was $400," he says. "Then the next year I got a scholarship just as the war broke out. I joined the Marine Corps and spent four years with them. I was in Pearl Harbor after it was bombed and then I went to Saipan, Tinian, and Iwo Jima. We were on the way to Japan when the war ended. I went back to school, finished my senior year, and finally came to New York in 1948."

"When I got here it was all different," he continues, laughing. "Suddenly the little fish was in the big pond and it was rough." He went to work right away, though. One day while passing the Broadhurst Theatre, he saw people going in to read for a production of *Romeo and Juliet* with Olivia DeHaviland. "I had this awful southern accent but

I decided to read anyway," he says. "Well, I got a one-line part. That was my first job in New York. The production only lasted six weeks but that wasn't Olivia's fault. I was thrilled to be making $85 a week and I was able to join the union as well."

What has the life of an actor been like? "Well, it's rough," Johnson admits. "It's like a curse because if it's in your blood, there's nothing you can do about it. I've had a lot of part-time jobs. But then I've had a lot of good jobs as well. I've worked steadily in recent years and done some minor movies and television. I did a lot of the soaps but those days are gone. I don't know how anybody does it now. Back then you could go off to summer stock and find out what acting is all about. Or else join the chorus. Actors can't do that anymore. They have no place to train. As for myself, it's been worth it. I'd do it again in a minute."

Incredibly, Johnson has lived at 49 Grove Street since 1950. "It used to be if you didn't have the rent the landlord would say, 'That's okay. Pay it next month,'" he recalls. "The West Village was wonderful. It was cheap! At Fedora's you could eat dinner for $4.95. All kinds of people came in and ate there. The subway was a nickel. You could go down to the end of Christopher Street to catch a ferry and ride back and forth to Hoboken. That was great on a summer night. The Theatre DeLys on Christopher Street was a movie theatre and on Tuesday nights they would hand out dishes."

And how has his life in the neighborhood changed over the years? "I live by myself with my two cats and still run around the Village on my bike. I used to go to dance class but don't do that much anymore. But casting agents still say I don't look my age. And I still think I'm young!"

Summing it up, Johnson sees the special character of the West Village as a perfect fit with his personal philosophy of life. "Treat everybody as you like to be treated," he states. "And you need a sense of humor. People are too serious these days. We used to all laugh and joke with each other." Yet after more than six decades here, Johnson doesn't hesitate when saying, "Even though it's changed and progress has set in, I wouldn't want to live anywhere else."

West Village Original • Film & Television

Karen Kramer

December 2017

Photo: Jessie Gladdek

Documentary filmmaker Karen Kramer's works include "The Jolo Serpent Handlers", "Rice and Peas", "Coney Island Mermaid", "Children of Shadows", and "The Ballad of Greenwich Village". Westchester-raised Kramer received her B.F.A. in film from NYU's Tisch School of the Arts. In addition to her film work, she is a freelance writer whose articles have appeared in multiple publications.

When documentary filmmaker Karen Kramer was in high school, she announced to her parents that she wasn't going to college. Instead, "hitchhiking around and having adventures" was what she planned to do. "Needless to say, that didn't go over too well with them," Kramer says, laughing. "So, I compromised and chose a university in Denver. It didn't seem tame like the suburbs where I grew up. I only lasted a year out there, though, and when I decided to leave Denver and settle down, I chose the one place on the planet that represented freedom to me. That place, of course, was Greenwich Village."

Kramer made the move here and attended NYU as a film major, eventually discovering that documentary films suited her best. "I had first wanted to be a writer," she says. "But I soon realized I wanted something bigger than writing. Film was a better medium for communicating my interest in other cultures and I started leaning toward documentaries. I had always been influenced by the work of Maya Deren, Storm de Hirsch, and Chick Strand and the more I studied, the more I knew I didn't want to do fiction films."

Her first documentary came about when a fellow film student asked her to travel to West Virginia to introduce his high school students to experimental films. "I agreed, but my one demand was that he take me to a snake-handling church while there," Kramer says. "I was very interested in ecstatic religion and rituals and had an idea to do films about that. I got to West Virginia with my windup Bolex and I filmed snake handlers, turning it into a 40-minute documentary called *The Jolo Serpent Handlers*. After that I was on my way to making films about cultures I found fascinating." Forty years and thirteen films later, Kramer still gets satisfaction from compliments about her sensitivity to the people that she films. "I think it's great that people recognize it because I work very hard at that," she says. "It would have been easy to make the Jolo serpent handlers look bad. Instead, I showed them at their best and let them speak in their own words. I think that's the secret to a good documentary."

Kramer's latest film is called *Renegade Dreamers*. It began from her fascination with the legendary Village coffee houses like the Gaslight and Figaro when there was an explosion of music and poetry that reverberated around the world. "I was curious to see if there were any people today following in those traditions," she says. "And I actually came across some wonderful radical songwriters and spoken-word artists who are on fire and using their own words today in the same way that people like Dylan and Ginsberg did back then. The film cuts back and forth between the past and the present and even though it's the older generation that gives it weight, it's the younger generation that gives it that arc."

Having lived on Leroy Street for decades, Kramer claims it's been a joyful experience. "Oh my God! It's a fantastic little street," she enthuses. "I have to say—without sounding corny—that I feel so grateful that I moved into this part of the Village when I did and experienced part of the old Italian flavor. You still had Borgia coffee house, you still had shops like Zito's Bread, fish stores, vegetable stores, and shops full of things that people really needed. I know that in some way it has really formed a piece of me."

"I feel really lucky to be here," she continues. "Every time I think about leaving the Village and living elsewhere, I realize that even with all its problems, the Village is much better than anywhere else. It's the people in New York that I love. The type of people: they're alert and awake. These days a lot of us are saying, 'This isn't the New York I used to know.' But still we don't leave. Perhaps that's because we really want to be here after all."

West Village Original • Film & Television

Joe Lisi
January 2015

Actor and former policeman Joe Lisi was born in Greenpoint, Brooklyn in 1950. After a 24-year career in the New York City police department–rising to the rank of captain–Lisi went into acting full-time. He has appeared in such TV series as "Third Watch" from 2000-2005, "True Blue" and "The Sopranos," as well as on and off-Broadway. Lisi lives with his wife, Donna, on West 10th Street near Hudson.

Photo: Curtis Holbrook

While he was growing up in Queens, Joe Lisi wanted to be both a New York City cop and an actor. "I'm sure I wanted to be a cop because I loved watching Robert Stack in *The Untouchables* on television. With the crowd I hung out with, everyone wanted to be Al Capone but I wanted to be Elliott Ness," he says, laughing. "I liked helping people. I tell everyone that if you like helping people, being a cop is the best job in the world."

When Lisi turned 29, he began to study acting at HB Studio on Bank Street and for a number of years, his police and acting career coincided. "Even though I didn't know what an audition was, I first tried out for a local community theatre production of *Arsenic and Old Lace* in Queens," he says. "Of course, they cast me as one of the cops!" At the same time, Lisi was promoted to sergeant. "Now I had a team of detectives that I worked with," he says. "They looked at me like I was a bit nuts because I would have them run lines with me. They were very supportive, though. The people in the police department thought that I was an ultra-liberal because I had friends who were actors, and the people in the artistic community thought I was just to the right of Attila the Hun, because I was a cop! I straddled both worlds and it was a lot of fun to do that."

Are there any similarities between being a policeman and acting? "Actually, in many ways there are," Lisi replies. "If you're undercover—

as I was—then you're always posing as someone else. When cops are on patrol they're involved in different situations where they often have to use talents and characteristics that are not truly their own, many times to avoid escalating a situation. So the job definitely does entail some acting. Not in a formal way, of course, but it certainly helped me in my training to be an actor."

According to Lisi, what he likes best about acting is the opportunity to entertain people. "Everybody has problems going on in their lives," he says. "So when they go to the theater, see a movie, or even watch TV, they're able to put all that stress on the back burner and just enjoy themselves for a few hours. I think it's great to be able to do that for people. That's one of the reasons I like it so much. And, of course, I have a big ego as well." He laughs. "I have to confess!"

As a long-time resident of the West Village, Lisi is most disappointed about the changes that have come to Bleecker Street. "Most of those small businesses are gone," he says. "One of the most recent ones to disappear was Manatus Restaurant. My wife and I, we loved that place! It was the perfect place to take visiting friends for a quick breakfast. From what I understood, the only reason they left was because the landlord raised the rent so much. It's happening all over and, as far as Bleecker Street is concerned, I have no reason to go into those new stores. That's the shame of it." Lisi pauses for a second. "But then I think of my Dad, who lived to be 93 and had an unbelievable capacity to accept change," he continues. "He just rolled with the punches. Maybe that's a less stressful way to go about it."

"Besides, I think it's still a great place to live and a wonderful place to raise children," Lisi says. "The West Village really does have a great sense of community. The core of people that live here are all very friendly. It's like a small town that way." And one last thing he feels is unique is the environment. "There's all kinds of people and all kinds of opinions here," he says. "It prepares you for the realities of life later on. Life can be difficult at times, but I think you're more prepared for it if you've been fortunate enough to grow up in a neighborhood like this."

West Village Original • Film & Television

Victor Mignatti
October 2008

Photo: Michael Mayers

Filmmaker Victor Mignatti is the Grammy Award-nominated director of the 2008 Billboard #1 pop-culture phenomenon R. Kelly's "Trapped in the Closet," distributed by IFC. He is also the writer-director of the award-winning feature film "Broadway Damage," director of "The Real World New Orleans," and numerous television programs, reality specials, and pilots.

For Victor Mignatti, the West Village is where his heart has been for nearly three decades. After a recent nine-and-a-half-year stint in Los Angeles, the Philadelphia-born filmmaker is back in New York and currently resides on Greenwich Avenue. As Mignatti explains, "The West Village has been my spiritual home since I was 17. That's when I came to NYU to study film between my junior and senior years in high school. Back then the West Village was far more dark and adventurous. Since that time, I've seen some wonderful changes and some upsetting changes in this neighborhood. But it's still a great neighborhood and I find that New York remains warm, engaging, and funny."

In 1994 Mignatti moved to Los Angeles for work reasons, returning to New York on a permanent basis again in 2004. However, he never gave up his New York driver's license or his West Village address. "I felt like a California license would be betraying New York," Mignatti laughs. He does, though, have some nice things to say about the Los Angeles experience. "I love Los Angeles," he admits. "It's a great place in terms of quality of home life. Also, it's easier to be an artist there financially than in New York right now. I lived in a beautiful house that I paid less for than my apartment here in the West Village." However, it was the differences from New York that started to weigh on Mignatti. "What was hard for me about Los Angeles is that it's very isolating and lonely because Angelenos are separated by their automobiles," he says.

"I've never found New York to be like that. Here everyone is sitting shoulder to shoulder on the subway. And at the end of day I felt like I belonged in a pedestrian city with a sensibility more rooted in European traditions, so I moved back to New York."

Mignatti's newest project is a feature music documentary entitled *This Time*. It follows the careers of six recording artists, including the legendary Sweet Inspirations who started as a stand-alone female group in the 60s and went on to be backup singers for performers like Aretha Franklin and Elvis Presley. As the artists attempt to make peace with the disappointments of their pasts, they continue to pursue their dreams. What emerges is a funny, heartwarming, and beautifully edited tribute to the indomitable human spirit. "The project started because I was friends with Peitor Angell who produced music for TV commercials I've directed," Mignatti recounts. "He told me he was producing the Sweet Inspirations' first album in 23 years. I thought it sounded interesting and suggested I come over one day with my video camera and film it. Initially, I thought I could do a promotional piece for him. But after a couple of days, I realized it had the potential for being a wonderful feature documentary and I kept shooting."

Alas, it's a constant challenge to raise money and it's only become more difficult with the current climate on Wall Street. In fact, Mignatti says that what separates the men from the boys in the world of filmmaking are those who can raise the money versus those who can't. And if you can't do it, you're not going to be a filmmaker. "It's very frustrating and painful at times," he admits. "But the joy of sitting in a theatre and feeling an audience emotionally involved with your film, well, there's nothing like it. The rewards are tremendous if you can stick with it."

Does he have any final thoughts on being an artist in the West Village? "I don't feel New York is as inspiring as it used to be," Mignatti says. "Everything is too sanitized. But perhaps that's because I've been here so long. I do think it's very different than it was thirty years ago socio-economically. Today's West Village artists are people who've achieved a certain level of financial success in their field. It's not a place for struggling artists and I think that's a major historical shift. It's still a place for artists, but artists of a certain financial caliber. It's interesting. Very interesting."

West Village Original • Film & Television

Sybil Sage
November 2012

Writer and artist Sybil Sage was one of the first women to write for TV comedies, listing "The Mary Tyler Moore Show," "Rhoda" and "Maude" among her many credits. She has lived for years at 45 Christopher Street with her husband, Martin, and these days she runs a successful business creating and selling her beautiful pique assiette pieces. You can buy them at www.sybilsage.com.

Photo: Robert Wright

"It's one of the coldest places ever," Sybil Sage says of her hometown, Winnipeg, Manitoba. "It was 50 below and it's prairie. My parents were born in Russia and they probably went to Canada because they had family there. At some point, they realized there was a life beyond Winnipeg so we moved to New Jersey and then New York. I grew up in Teaneck. It's okay to be from those places if you can end up in Greenwich Village!" she says, laughing.

Sage majored in psychology at NYU but fell into the entertainment business one summer while visiting her brother in Los Angeles. She started working as a secretary for Carl Reiner, who had begun producing a TV series called *The New Dick Van Dyke Show*. "I had always liked writing but it seemed very lofty to me," Sage says. "However, working with Carl, I met the writers and it became less intimidating. They weren't exactly Chaucer or Shakespeare. Actually, they were the kind of guys you wouldn't go out with in high school. But they all looked very rich and I thought, 'Hmmm, maybe this is something!'"

One night, Sage was watching *The Mary Tyler Moore Show* when she decided to write a spec script for the series. "It was a time when there were more shows starring interesting women characters," she recalls. "But there were very few women writers. I teamed up with a friend, Barbara Gallagher, and we started getting a lot of work.

It's possible we were the first female writing team in TV. It turns out that the shows that appreciated having women writers did benefit from them."

Sage moved back to New York in the 1970s, got married and in 1980, moved to the Village. "We knew that there wouldn't be much TV work in New York for us but we wanted to raise our son here," she says. "I wanted a New York kid. I wasn't sure about raising a kid in the Village but it turns out he loved it. There's life here and it's exciting and there's diversity. You've got to walk the walk if you want a kid to feel a part of the world and that was hard to do in Los Angeles."

Several years ago, Sage was ready to try something new when she took a class in *pique assiette*, a form of art similar to mosaic but which specifically uses broken plates and the like arranged in patterns or designs. "I just got passionate about it," she says. "Nuts about it, really. There was no stopping me. I was doing it to anything that was standing still: vases, picture frames, pencil holders, you name it. I even got into cremation urns, for both pets and people!" What is it about the process that Sage enjoys? "It's very creative," she replies. "It's a little bit like comedy writing because you're creating a character and you can personalize it. I turn the mosaic into a story about somebody. And it's fun for people who order them as gifts because they get to participate. It's very collaborative."

As a longtime West Villager, Sage has had a front row seat to the changes here. "There are some places that I still miss, like Rumbles Bakery," she says, laughing. "And as you know, the designers discovered Bleecker Street so now there are $1,200 boots in shop windows. An Italian clothing shop just opened at the corner of Bleecker and Bank. The first time I looked at the prices, they were so high I asked the staff if they were in lira! There didn't used to be anything unaffordable in the Village and now there is. That was surprising."

"I'm a little worried about NYU building those high rises as well," she continues. "But on a happier note, the High Line is gorgeous! I walk along the Hudson and they now have sailing and golf in addition to everything else. I feel like it's the best of the country and the city. I don't know why anyone goes away for the weekend because it's all here. There's nothing you can't do here. It really is like heaven on earth. I'm not worried about whether there's an afterlife because I can't imagine it being any better than this."

West Village Original • Film & Television

Richard Eric Weigle
October 2017

Richard Eric Weigle is organizer and host of the third annual Greenwich Village Film Festival, screening at Greenwich House. Born in Scotch Plains, NJ, in 1945, Weigle has had a variety of careers including–for the past 17 years–president of the Grove Street Block Association. He has lived on Grove Street for 44 years and currently resides there with his husband, interior designer Michael Anastasio.

In the course of Richard Weigle's long and varied career he spent two years as a Peace Corps volunteer in the Philippines, taught school for 25 years, had a recurring role on television's *Guiding Light*, served as director of the library at the Museum of Television and Radio, and was an associate producer on the documentary film *Broadway: The Golden Age*.

"I had always been interested in film but never dreamed that I could become a film producer," Weigle says. "That's why when I heard there was going to be a Greenwich Village film festival—started by the actors and directors Antonio Padovan and Alessia Gatti—I became so enamored of the idea. I went to producer Rick McKay, whom I had met through my work at the museum, and suggested that we put together a small film to enter." The resulting 20-minute film was called *Greenwich Village: A World Apart* and featured actors talking about theatre and living in the Village.

Not only did he submit a film, but Weigle also became determined to help the organizers bring the festival to the next level. "The first film festival was just one night at the Players Theatre," he says. "I've had a long tenure as president of my block association so I know everybody in the neighborhood. Along with my husband, Michael, I got started by raising money and facilitating contacts. We helped them take the festival to three nights last year. This year it will run for four nights and hopefully it will keep growing."

As for the festival's premise, Weigle says they're trying to bring back the Village as a center for creativity and the arts. "It's such an iconic place but it's getting a reputation for being gentrified," he says. "This area has a rich history of individualism and was once the center of the beat generation, folk music, the arts, and protest. I think we have as many creative people here as we ever did, we just need venues where they can show their work." And right now the festival is a labor of love; no one is making any money from it. "If you do everything for money, you're going to miss out on so much," Weigle says. "My mother once said, 'Richard, you will never lose that Peace Corp spirit.'" He laughs. "But I don't care! I do it because I want to be inspired and I want to be inspiring."

Weigle moved to Grove Street in 1973 and has witnessed enormous changes first-hand. "When I moved here it was 80% gay and now it's 80% straight," he says. "That's one major difference! And you can't help but see the steep price of housing, the increase in rents, or the small businesses that were forced out. But a lot of things also happened for the better when the West Village became gentrified. It has never looked nicer, the street lamps have been replaced with period crook lamps, there's a big increase in trees and plants, and it's never been safer. Those are huge things."

"I actually don't talk a lot about the 'good old days'," he continues. "Yes, there were things that were great then but I really believe in embracing the present and trying to find solutions to current problems. When people ask me how I run such a successful block association, I say you can do one of two things. If you don't want to work then write a check and if you don't have money, then do some work. But do something for the community! That's my philosophy."

Speaking for both himself and his husband, Weigle admits, "We love New York. We're not happy about the current political climate in this country but here it's still very tolerant and open-minded. From the moment I moved onto Grove Street, it was clear that no one cared about your race, your religion, your sexuality, your college, or what your parents did. It was 'Tell me about yourself right now.' That's the way the Village has always been for me and always will be. It's about tolerance."

West Village Original • Journalism

James Lincoln Collier

May 2011

Journalist and author James Lincoln Collier was born in New York City in 1928. While probably best known these days for his still-successful children's novels, Collier sees himself primarily as a humorist and has published many articles in that genre. A resident of Barrow Street for the past forty years, Collier is also an accomplished jazz musician who plays the trombone professionally.

"I come from a family of writers," says James Lincoln Collier. "My father was a writer and an editor, mostly of pulp westerns. He came from an old New England family but he ran away and ended up working as a cowboy on cattle ranches out West. Henry David Thoreau had been in love with his grandmother, Ellen Sewell, so there was a kind of literary way of thinking in the family because of that connection. In addition, my uncle and e.e. cummings became very close friends when they met in Europe during World War I while in the Ambulance Corps. Hart Crane was also very close to my family. In 1925 my parents bought a summer cottage in Pawling—which I now own—and all of those literary people used to go up and have parties and drink a great deal."

One would think that with such a pedigree, Collier would have naturally taken up writing himself. But it took him a while to decide on that as a career. "I wasn't drawn to it particularly," he admits. "I think in a way I had seen too much of it. There were always writers around the house and none of them ever had any money. And they were never a particularly cheerful bunch. It was only when I was leaving the army and finally starting my life that I thought to myself 'now what?'"

That's when it came to Collier that he was, indeed, going to write. "I didn't look forward to that career with great joy, but it just seemed I was fated to do so," he says. "So I tried to make a go of it. I got a job, got married, had kids, and all the time I was writing. After a while I realized I could do it, so I quit my day job and started freelancing. By that time, I was really cranking out the magazine articles at a great rate. For 25 years I guess I was one of the busiest magazines writers in the country. I did all right and supported my family quite well."

Mixing his love of jazz music and playing, Collier also began writing books about jazz. "I had a great deal of success with that," he says. "I wrote *The Making of Jazz,* and it was one of the most successful books ever on the subject, as well as a finalist for the National Book Award. Then I did a series of biographies of jazz musicians for Oxford."

For Collier, what turned out to be the best part of writing was the research. "If you're going to do a proper job as a writer, you've got to do the research," he says. "You can't fake it. I was always careful to make sure I had done my homework. In those days magazines had the money to send their writers around so I was traveling a lot as well. I interviewed all the top people in their fields as a result and ended up learning a great deal. That part of it was really very interesting."

When asked how the Village has changed in the course of his lifetime, Collier is quick to reply. "It's very simple. It used to be cheap!" he says, laughing. "Back in the 50s you could get apartments for $25 a month. These were small apartments, mind you, but cheap rents meant that the Village housed the kind of people who were drawn here because of its reputation as a haunt for artists and writers. Then the rents all began to go up in the late 80's and people like that had to move out." Now he feels the landlords are running everything. "There's never been any sense that the Village had a certain tradition or ambiance to be maintained," he says. "The real estate people are just looking for the biggest buck they can get and nowadays the person who can afford that isn't the guy sitting home writing his novel."

Nevertheless, Collier says he still feels at home here. "I feel this is a natural, comfortable place for me to be," he says. "My dad and mother lived on Waverly Place for a while, and my uncle and aunt were also in the Village. My boys grew up here. So the family has had someone in the Village for about 100 years. Physically it still looks almost the same as it always has and I think I'll probably stay here."

West Village Original • Journalism

Mimi Sheraton

June 2010

Food editor and writer Mimi Sheraton was the restaurant critic for the New York Times from 1975-83. Her columns have appeared in countless magazines including Harper's Bazaar, Vogue, Esquire, The New York Times Magazine, and Condé Nast Traveler. She lives on West 12th Street with her husband, Richard Falcone, in the brownstone they bought 45 years ago.

While she was growing up in the Midwood section of Brooklyn, Mimi Sheraton soon discovered that not all food was alike with regards to quality. "My mother was a very good cook," she recalls. "It was very important to her. My father was in the wholesale fruit and produce business in Washington Market. He would come home and talk a great deal about fruit and produce from different places. As a young person, I quickly got to know that there was such a thing as discernment when it came to food. Though I wasn't aware of it at the time, I think it made me conscious of that all my life."

After graduating from NYU with a major in journalism and marketing, Sheraton first began writing about interior design and home furnishing. "I never knew there was such a profession or career as writing about food," she says. It was while she was working as the home editor at *Seventeen* that she was asked if she would like to be the food editor as well. "Everyone knew I liked food and could cook," Sheraton says. "So it was a very easy transition to food writing. And I liked it better. There was a lot of freelance work in it as well as a lot of travel."

In 1975, Sheraton landed what some might think is the ultimate job for a food writer: restaurant critic for *The New York Times*. And what was that like? "I loved it," she admits. "It was a lot of pressure and a lot of eating, but I loved doing it. I'm crazy about restaurants and I thought it was fun and useful to be doing the critiquing. Of course, New York is a great city to do it in because of the diversity of restaurants. There are big fancy ones, interesting humble ones, and almost every kind of cuisine in the world. So it was a very interesting job." Sheraton subsequently quit the *Times* in 1983 for a couple of reasons. "Some were having to do with politics at the paper," she says. "But I also felt that I was becoming too well known in New York to do restaurant reviewing anonymously, which is the only way it can be done valuably." Still, it remains the job she claims to have loved the most.

Sheraton first moved to the Village in 1945 while attending college. "It was much quieter then, more laid back, maybe a little more Bohemian," she remembers. "The Village was a place of human proportions with very liberal people. It was also a very contentious population, which I like: people always fighting for their rights and fighting to preserve the neighborhood."

What are some of the biggest changes Sheraton has seen in the Village? "Prices!" she says, laughing. "But seriously, affordability for young people and artists has changed a great deal and with that came a change in the population too. The advent of co-ops and condos means we have wealthier people coming to buy the property. Unfortunately, they're not quite as laid back as the old Villagers used to be." Sheraton also has harsh words for her alma mater. "I hate NYU because they're destroying Greenwich Village," she says. "I've lived here 65 years, I'm a property owner, and I deplore what NYU is doing to the Village. I'm not at all proud of being a graduate. And you can put that in the article!"

Sheraton remains committed to the Village, though. As befits a food enthusiast, she recites a long list of local restaurants that she enjoys patronizing, from Babbo to Elephant & Castle. And she has nice words to say about the Sixth Precinct as well, claiming to have a lot of faith in them. Summing up a successful life and career in this neighborhood, she says, "I'm as delighted to be living here as I was when I first moved in. The minute I discovered the Village and roamed around it, I wanted to live here. And over the years, the Village has been very good to me."

West Village Original • Journalism

Calvin Trillin

May 2009

Journalist, humorist, and novelist Calvin Trillin was born in Kansas City in 1935. After a stint in the U.S. army, Trilin worked as a reporter for Time Magazine before joining the staff of The New Yorker in 1963. He was also a regular contributor to The Nation, as well as being a renowned writer on cuisine. He moved to New York City in 1961 and has been a resident of the West Village since 1969.

When writer Calvin Trillin moved to Grove Street in 1969, partitioning Greenwich Village into even smaller areas was not common. "I've never known to this day where the 'West Village' is," he admits. "When I moved here I'm not sure the phrase was used very much. I might be wrong about that, but if it had been used I would've thought it meant west of Hudson. I always thought I lived in Greenwich Village and didn't know I lived in the West Village."

Growing up in Kansas City, Trillin made it east when he attended Yale University, eventually becoming a writer and chairman of the Yale Daily News. A career as an author was quite a departure from the family business. In fact, his father was a grocer. "He started with a little store," he recalls. "He didn't go to college himself, but he decided he wanted his son to go to Yale. I never knew how he paid for my college tuition until after he died. It happened that in his first store there was a bread company that gave you a 2% rebate if you displayed their bread and paid your bill on time. It was that rebate money—which he put away for years—that paid for my tuition at Yale." After graduating, Trillin did a stint in the army, worked in the Atlanta bureau of Time Magazine, and then settled permanently in New York when Time transferred him here.

When Trillin and is wife, Alice, moved to the West Village, it was with the idea of trying something new. "At that time," he recounts, "the custom of converting the commercial and industrial structures west of Hudson Street into residential buildings hadn't really started. It just wasn't a common thing then. My wife and I looked at a sort of stable on Washington Street with the idea of turning it into a house. That, however, was a truly cockamamie scheme and luckily we didn't do it!" They eventually settled in a town house on Grove Street. "Back then, the Village looked about the same as it does now," Trillin says. "Since this part of the Village is a historic district, changing facades is difficult. As a result, there are still a lot of people making movies here because you can get the 1890's or the 1930s look very easily."

Recalling the Village of those days, Trillin says, "It was obviously a little funkier then." But it was also easier to do certain things. "I remember when my girls and I first ran into the Halloween Parade," he says. "We didn't even know about it. They just passed us on the street and there were a couple of hundred people in great costumes. There was also a small police presence so we could get in and out of the parade at will. I think it's difficult now to have that kind of neighborhood event. With hyper-communication and a lot of people able to move around quickly, it's almost impossible to have a little community event that doesn't become either too large or get crushed." On the other hand, there are some things that have greatly improved the quality of life in the neighborhood. "When I first moved here we didn't have, of course, the park along the Hudson. Now it's a wonderful water park and my grandchildren adore it."

On the subject of neighborhood as destiny, Trillin lays his success firmly at the feet of the Village. "I always thought I couldn't really have made it uptown," he says, laughing. "I think the Village is full of people like me who are from the rest of the country. In a way, it's more like where we came from than the rest of Manhattan because it's mostly low-rise. You can actually see the sun and you're likely to have a next-door neighbor instead of someone you just see in the elevator. It's less formal as well. I once talked to a historian at NYU who said that was true even of the early Village bohemians; many of them were from small towns. They felt more comfortable in the Village. For people who come from the rest of the country, it just seems like a more natural place."

West Village Original • Journalism

Nancy Weber
May 2012

Journalist and author Nancy Weber is known primarily for her non-fiction work "The Life Swap." Her twenty-some other books include "The Playgroup" and "Brokenhearted," as well as eight romances written under the byline Jennifer Rose. Currently residing on West Tenth Street, Weber also caters parties and teaches cooking.

While growing up in Hartford, Connecticut, writer Nancy Weber was fortunate enough to have parents who were intent on exposing her and her brother to everything New York City had to offer. "I perfectly remember the moment when I was a teenager and we had just seen *The Boy Friend* at the Cherry Lane Theatre," she recalls. "There was something about that curve of Commerce Street that brought me to my knees and I said to my parents, 'I'm going to have to live here when I grow up.' And they didn't laugh at me!"

Not only didn't they laugh, her parents were instrumental in landing Weber her first Village apartment. "I was attending Sarah Lawrence College but I wanted to drop out," she explains. "My parents offered me the 'princess deal' of all times. Since I hated living in the dorms, they suggested I live in Greenwich Village and commute up to school and get my degree that way. So I agreed to it! I ended up on Seventh Avenue South in a triangular apartment and it was total bliss. That was the spring of 1962 and I've been in the Village ever since."

Looking for work as a writer after graduating, Weber landed the "best of all possible first jobs." "I was editorial assistant on the amusement desk of the *New York Post*," she says. "That meant that I was working with guys like Jerry Tallmer, Richard Watts, and Archer Winston and copy editing Earl Wilson." After a while she began writing for the paper herself, getting the chance to interview Francois Truffaut and Norman Mailer, among others. From here it was on to numerous books and a life's devotion to the written word. "I just love making sentences," Weber confesses. "When I'm writing fiction I adore hanging out with my characters. There's that incredible sense, familiar to so many fiction writers, that you're not so much creating events as remembering them." She goes on to articulate the difference for her between writing fiction and non-fiction. "I think it's very hard for journalists to write fiction because you have to give yourself permission to lie in a way. You have to make things up. There's something beautiful about facts. And yet making things up or remembering things that didn't actually happen is a gorgeous experience."

Does she still remember what the Village was like when she moved into her first apartment? "It was much as it is today," Weber observes. "It was this little pocket of coziness and warmth. It was so livable, and it still is. I think what I loved most is that it was not homogenous. If we were homogenous it was for reasons of affinity and not because of our backgrounds or our religion or how much money we had. I still feel that heady air of freedom that I first did moving here."

While many people would bemoan the changes in the neighborhood, Weber offers another perspective. "I'm the wrong person to ask how the Village has changed," she admits. "It has always seemed like a place that was sort of in flux and that's the point of being here. The Village is about change and even though there are certain things that you hope to have preserved, you don't want everything frozen in amber, either. I can get a little impatient if people go on about life not being the same because you can't get a croissant at Sutter's any more. While I can certainly mourn the loss of St. Vincent's and I guess NYU is a real estate monster, I'm not going to dance at the preservation ball. Some things are going to remain and some things are going to change."

When asked if she has any last words to say about the West Village, Weber laughingly replies, "This isn't my obit, is it?" Then she grows thoughtful. "I can't imagine getting tired of it," she says. "I guess it's too late to say I want to grow old here, having just turned 70. I have to say, 'Damn it, I *did* grow old here!' I found my magic spot. I just feel so lucky. I think whatever changes come here we will roll with them and the Village will go on being the garden spot of the universe."

When you live in the West Village you get a chance to hold on to a bit more of the charm of life. And I think the most charming part of New York is the West Village, hands down.

—Denise Marsa

Gay Street

West Village Original • Music

David Amram

February 2014

Composer, conductor, and author David Amram was born in Philadelphia in 1930. He's written over 100 orchestral and chamber music works, as well as Broadway musicals, operas, and scores for such films as "Splendor in the Grass" and "The Manchurian Candidate." David is the subject of the recent documentary film entitled "David Amram: The First 80 Years."

When David Amram was a boy, his parents decided to work for the war effort. So they moved the family from a 160-acre farm in Pennsylvania to a tiny house in Washington, D.C. "It was what they called a 'checkerboard' neighborhood because black and white folks lived together," he says. "In 1942, D.C. was still officially segregated except for a few areas such as ours. As a result, I was surrounded by all kinds of incredible music: gospel, church, jazz, and the blues. It was all part of the neighborhood experience." Amram was already studying classical musical but this exposure opened up the world of jazz to him as well and he decided to pursue both.

After high school, Amram attended Oberlin College. At that time, school policy forbade anyone to play jazz in the piano room. "When I told the music department that I wanted to play jazz AND write symphonies, they thought I had a mental problem and tried to discourage me," he says, laughing. "While I appreciated their sincerity, I wanted the option to fail at something before I gave up. And it was good to have that experience because it taught me about what it takes to be an artist. It's a lifetime pursuit and it takes very hard work."

Amram's latest piece, *Greenwich Village Portraits*, is a testament to this fortitude. "I worked tremendously hard on this piece," he says. "I wanted to use it as a way to honor the people and streets of a fantastic neighborhood in a great city that's given so many of us a life that we never would have had. That's what kept me going to finish it. The beautiful thing about a composition is that you're trying to build some-thing that has value and is meant to last. Not as an ego trip, but as a thank you note for being alive and to all the people who are no longer here."

Amram moved to the City in 1955 then, two years later, to 114 Christopher Street. "The Village was wonderful then," he remembers. "A real community. I was constantly meeting these amazing people and having wonderful conversations. I met so many artists of all mediums who had (barely) lived through the Depression. Somehow they had managed to not only find a way to pursue their dreams, but then went out of their way to encourage a young hayseed like myself to dare to pursue mine as well."

And what about the vast changes to the neighborhood over the years? "People say nowadays that the Village isn't really the Village anymore," Amram says. "But when they do I ask them, 'What would O'Henry say if he came back and saw how Washington Square has changed? Or what would Edna St. Vincent Millay say?' I guess it's part of growing old to say, 'Things just ain't what they used to be.' But they never are!"

Besides, Amram feels that rather than screaming the blues, artists should be the ones passing on that wonderful history. "Right now, it's 'full greed ahead' in the Village," he says. "But if you preserve its spirit, people will find that it can still exist here. We're not going to let this legacy die because some people who are culturally and spiritually deprived have suddenly taken charge. It's our gig to be respectful to them—they have to support their families after all—but at the same time we have to show others there's an alternative and not assume this is the way it has to be."

Amram hasn't lived in the Village since 1994, when his landlord was able to successfully evict him from his rent-controlled apartment. Since then, he's made his home up in the Putnam Valley. However, this neighborhood still has a hold on him. "When I come back to the Village to play in a club, I think of how lucky I am to have been here in 1955 and to still be here now," he says. "If I hit the lottery and became a multimillionaire I'd move back to the Village in a minute. That's because I love it. It's really one of my homes as long as I'm alive. "

West Village Original • Music

Bill Curreri
November 2014

Bill Curreri was born in St. Vincent's Hospital in 1949. After successful careers in pharmaceutical marketing and academia, Curreri began a new one as a musician with the release of his first album in 2012. His second album, "Son of An American Dream," has just been released and is generating considerable radio play internationally. Bill has lived on Leroy Street most of his life.

"I was always in love with music," admits singer-songwriter Bill Curreri. "My first exposure to it was sitting in my grandfather's lap and listening to Neapolitan music. Then I got into opera, movie scores and, as a teenager, Doo-wop music. And growing up in the Village during the folk era, well, that music really hooked me. In the 60s this neighborhood was teeming, just teeming, with musicians!"

While Curreri spent his early years immersed in the local music scene, including a stint as a singer in his brother's band called "The Village Merchants," his life took a couple of detours. After a successful career in pharmaceutical marketing and advertising Curreri felt he was finally ready to launch his music career. Then, in 2000, he got a phone call from a friend.

"He begged me to teach remedial reading classes at John Jay College and I agreed," Curreri says. "I loved it! I got a lot of satisfaction helping my students get to the next level. It paid nothing but it was probably the best 'job' I ever had. I did that for 12 years. Finally, one day I was talking to my partner, Lydia, about my music and she said, 'Maybe it's time for you to be a little selfish.' She was right. It was time for me. I reluctantly walked away from the kids but I thanked God for whatever good came out of it."

Through it all, Curreri had maintained an in-house recording studio and continued to write songs over the years. "I always had a reputation among the musicians I hung with as being a good songwriter," he says. "I also have a knack for a good melody and a solid hook for a chorus." All this came to fruition when he released his first album, *Long Time Gone*, in 2012 and now *Son of an American Dream*.

What does the new title mean? "First, it's a homage to my parents, grandparents, and large extended family," Curreri says. "They always encouraged us to get a good education and told us we could be anything we wanted to be in this country." Secondly, it's a call to younger people to get involved. "When we were kids we knew about current events," he says. "We were very much wrapped up in them and, in fact, our music was an expression of that. Now kids today can't even tell you who the Vice President is! I'm trying to tell them that in order to achieve your American dream you've got to get involved. You have to figure out for yourself what's going on in the world and who represents your values."

As a child of the Village, what changes resonate most with him? "Back then the Village was not as homogenous," Curreri remembers. "Our section was essentially an Italian ghetto and we called it 'the neighborhood.' However, if you crossed west on Seventh Avenue you were in a totally different Village. We thought the residents there were rich and well educated. Another thing was that the area was crawling with children. Every park, playground, and pool was packed with kids! That's probably the thing I miss the most. And, finally, I remember the mob influence in the Village. It was a fact of life and we all saw it. Some of the guys I grew up with were attracted to that life but they died young as a result. So the absence of that is definitely a change for the better."

And, of course, it was the arts and music in particular that defined the Village for Curreri and which he returns to. "Music was such a fundamental component of life here; you couldn't escape it," he says. "But it's not here today. Instead, the Village is losing its artistic heritage and becoming totally celebrity focused. In the short term, I'm not optimistic for its future." Then Curreri observes that the "pendulum" of life always swings back and forth. "I'm not discounting a day when the artistic heritage of the Village will return and bring others with it," he says. "Eventually this area will come back to its roots. As an old-time Village resident I think there's just too much heritage here that makes it so different from the rest of New York. I believe that artists of every ilk will always be attracted to the Village."

West Village Original • Music

David Del Tredici

October 2014

Photo: Maggie Berkvist

Pulitzer Prize-winning composer David Del Tredici was born in California in 1937. A former Guggenheim and Woodrow Wilson Fellow, he is considered a pioneer of the Neo-Romantic movement. His most recent composition is "Bullycide," which deals with gay teen suicide as a result of bullying. Del Tredici moved to New York City in the early 1960s and has been a resident of Westbeth since 1971.

As a child growing up in Cloverdale, California, composer David Del Tredici was aching for something artistic to do. Yet it took some time for him to discover just what that was. "I was an ardent flower arranger before music. My mother took me to classes with her. I used to enter competitions; all these old ladies and a ten-year-old boy!" he says, laughing. "It wasn't until I was about 12 that I began playing the piano. I started simply to get out of playing baseball with the bad boys who teased me. However, it turned out I had a talent for the piano. It became my obsession and by the time I was 17 I was performing recitals with the San Francisco Symphony."

It was while at the Aspen Music Festival—between his junior and senior years of college—that he wrote his very first piece. "I played it for Darius Milhaud who exclaimed, 'My boy, you are a composer!'" Del Tredici says. "With that validation, I went back to college and went into the graduate composition seminar."

When Del Tredici began composing, the prevailing idiom of the day was atonality. But in the late 60s he sat down to write *Final Alice*—based on Lewis Carroll's *Alice in Wonderland*—and something changed. "The words were so whimsical and witty of Victorian England," he says. "To reflect that I unselfconsciously had to grasp tonality. And little by little I introduced it into my composing vocabulary and I think I did it in an effective way. Now I'm called the father of neo-romanticism."

At the same time Del Tredici, being gay himself, found he was welcomed into a world of gay composers. "I met Aaron Copland in 1964 after I sent him a piano piece I had written. I was really cute and very talented and it was easy for me get along with the *hoi polloi* of gay composers," he says laughingly. "In that sense I had an advantage and I sailed right into that world. It seemed like all the great composers were queer! Menotti, Copland, Bernstein, Barber. It's way beyond the normal "one in ten" queer number." Why does he think that's the case? "In my generation it had to do with the pain of growing up in a society that despised you," Del Tredici posits. "When you found you had a talent for something it was a ticket to success and acceptance."

It would be years later, though, that Del Tredici finally came out, both personally and musically. That was also after being an alcoholic for ten years, which was a surprise to him. "I got everything I thought I wanted, including a Pulitzer Prize," he says. "But I relaxed and all the energy that had gone into striving went into drinking. Eventually, I realized it was eroding my energy to compose. In the process of recovery I found out a lot about myself and that allowed me to be more open about being gay. It also occurred to me to write music about being gay. That would be the ultimate creative 'outness'."

When asked what the neighborhood was like when he moved to Westbeth in 1971, Del Tredici replies enthusiastically. "It was wild," he says. "I loved it. There were sex clubs, leather clubs, and drag queens everywhere!" He laughs mischievously. "I had a great time and they were wild years for a gay man living in the West Village. I can't imagine who wouldn't have liked it!" But as gay people are being assimilated into society more and more, Del Tredici sees a disappearance of the culture he knew. "Young men aren't interested in the leather scene—which I think is also the history of the Village—or in impersonating women either," he says. "That has to do something to gay culture, at least as we knew it."

After logging in so many years in this part of town, can Del Tredici say he belongs? "I feel like a citizen of the Village, absolutely," he says. "I've lived in other places for a while but I always came back. Oh my God, this is the epicenter of culture and everything! The West Village really is the heart and soul of Manhattan. And I hope 'gayness' still fuels the creativity. I think that's still a big part of life here and in Manhattan as a whole."

West Village Original • Music

Bill Dunham

March 2013

Pianist Bill Dunham was born in Boston in 1928. Even though he always had a "day gig", for over 50 years he has appeared on Monday nights at Arthur's Tavern on Grove Street with his band, the Grove Street Stompers. Bill owns an apartment building on Barrow Street and these days he lives with his wife, Sonya, on the corner of 14th Street and Seventh Avenue.

During his high school years at Williston Academy in Massachusetts, Bill Dunham would hop a bus to the city of Worcester to take accordion lessons. To him, what was "beautiful" about that city was the Family Theatre on Main Street where they featured the big bands of the day. "After my accordion lessons I would go over to the Family Theatre and sit in the balcony," he says. "The theatre would go dark, the theme song of Les Brown's or Harry James' orchestra would start, the curtain would draw open, there they would be and—let me tell you—it was orgasmic. It was so exciting!"

At the same time Dunham was also taking piano lessons and while other kids were playing baseball, he was "grinding away" on the piano and hating it. "I had an old-fashioned music scroll that I would carry my music in and I looked like a kid out of Dickens," he explains. "Then I took lessons from a swing piano teacher at Williston and things changed. The spirit and the energy and the rhythm really got to me. My previous teacher had told me to put a dime on the back of my hand and not let it move when I played. When I started taking swing lessons this teacher said, 'For God sakes, get that dime off your hand and flop it around!'"

Dunham graduated from Williston in 1946 and joined the army. "I went to Korea where I was, among other things, a piano player in the regimental dance band," he says. Following his Army service,

Dunham attended Harvard on the G.I. Bill where he majored in economic theory as well as started a band. "We became the most popular traditional jazz band on the east coast," he says. "We played every big weekend at Dartmouth for five years. I spent so much time with this band that—I'm embarrassed to say—it took me five years to get out of Harvard instead of four!" And after a few years of working abroad, Dunham settled in New York in 1956 to continue his corporate career.

So how did the Grove Street Stompers come about? "In 1962 I started a band with a wonderful cornet player named Jimmy Gribbon," he recounts. "One day we walked into Arthur's Tavern on Grove Street and spoke to the owner—an irascible fellow named Jerry Maisano—who said we could play on Mondays for no pay. So we split the tip bowl and we've been there ever since. Every single Monday night for fifty years! Well, we closed for President Kennedy's funeral in 1963 and we also closed once for Jerry's funeral. And we've had four or five weather-related closings. And we never play New Years Eve. Other than that, we've been here every Monday night."

"When we started out at Arthur's we were pretty much an amateur jazz band," Dunham continues. "Our first bass player was a pilot for Eastern Airlines, for instance. The music wasn't that hot but the enthusiasm certainly was. But gradually over the years the band has transitioned to the point that it's now a professional band in terms of the musicians, who are pros. Except me. I'm still a rank amateur," he says, laughing. "I always had a day gig!"

What was the Village like back when he started at Arthur's? "It was quite different than it is now," he recalls. "Because rents were cheap, it was where artists and writers actually lived. They wrote, acted, and played, and this is where it all happened. For musicians there was a law that said you couldn't play in a place that served booze unless you had a cabaret license. So we all had to go to the police station to get finger printed. The Mafia controlled most of the bars and clubs back then as well, both straight and gay. They left Arthur's alone, though."

And even though the club was eventually sold, Dunham says that nothing has really changed there. "It's one of the last real 'joints' in town, which makes it kind of fun to play in," he says. "We've even managed over the years to increase our compensation somewhat. We actually get paid now!"

West Village Original • Music

Bobb Goldsteinn
November 2010

Showman, songwriter, and artist Bobb Goldsteinn is a pop pioneer who wrote The Village Stompers' international hit "Washington Square" in 1962. These days Goldsteinn is one of the founding members of The FOHQ (pronounced "folk") Club of Washington Square, which seeks to open a new hospital at Seventh Avenue at 12th Street now that St. Vincent's is gone.

"I come from two vast families," lyricist and artist Bobb Goldsteinn says. "On both my mother's and father's side there were approximately eleven siblings each. While both families were very accomplished, I was the first to go into entertainment, much to the dismay of them all. It was only after *Life* magazine did a story on me that my father embraced me for the first time in my life. That was on my thirtieth birthday."

Goldsteinn grew up in Philadelphia, where he attended high school on the west side. "I'm a proud graduate of Overbrook High School," he says. "In fact, I wrote 'Washington Square' while there. It was for a class project because the United Nations was just opening. I originally named the song 'India.' Madame Padit Nehru—who was the first ambassador from India to the UN—came to our school and gave me an award for writing it. Years later, I turned 'India' into 'Washington Square.' You can say I wrote my greatest song in high school and it's been downhill all the way!" He laughs. "Actually, it's been uphill all the way!" After high school, Goldsteinn spent two "desultory" years at Temple University, left to work in his uncle's bank for a while, headed to Provincetown for a summer, went back home to Philadelphia, and finally came to New York.

A chance encounter on New Years Eve in 1958 while in line to get into Lenny's on West 10th Street started Goldsteinn on his musical career. "I had just seen a musical called *Shoestring 57*," he recalls. "There were a couple of numbers in it that really took me; they were both melodic and very, very funny. So I'm talking to my date about the show and—I swear to God—this gentleman in front of us turns around and says 'I'm Claibe Richardson, the composer of those songs.' Amazing! When he found out that I was a lyricist—and found me very affable—he invited me to visit him and to show him some of my work. Three months later he recommended me for a summer project at the Tamiment Playhouse in the Poconos, and I got it. It was a dream project! I was 22, writing sketches with Woody Allen and writing songs with Billy Goldenberg. I have lived off of miracles all my life."

As he became a successful songwriter, Goldsteinn settled in the West Village and became involved in preserving it. "I marched with Jane Jacobs on three matters that threatened the Village in the early 1970s," he says. "The first one was to get William Zeckendorf to drop the idea of buying West Village Housing. Another time was getting Robert Moses to take his sticky fingers off of Broome Street, which he wanted to turn into a tunnel. That was Moses' last hurrah, as well as Zeckendorf's, and neither of them prevailed. These men retired in defeat. The last time was when the City allowed a reconditioned ferry to be placed at the end of Christopher Street as a methadone clinic. This was one initiative we weren't successful in blocking, and it ultimately blighted the Village."

These days, Goldsteinn cites two factors that threaten the existence of the Village as he used to know it. "Artists can't afford to live here when they're starting out their careers," he says. "That and NYU's expansion. Put those two together and they spell the end of the Village. They're taking away the certain peculiarities that gave it its flavor. I don't need to tell you that there are as many creative people as there used to be, not just as many struggling ones and I think that's sad."

Still, Goldstein professes his affection for the neighborhood, both for what it is and what it provided him. "I love the West Village," he says. "It's my history. While living here I accomplished all sorts of things. With the money I made from those ventures, I decided I wanted to move to Christopher Street so I could be one of those interesting people like in *Wonderful Town*. And I did. I know the Village will never be what it used to be, but I'm basically an optimist and I have great faith that it will continue to be special."

West Village Original • Music

Larry Ham
August 2009

Pianist, composer, and arranger Larry Ham has been long noted as a New York sideman performing, touring, and recording with many great jazz artists. He's now gaining new recognition as a solo artist with his latest CD release "Just Me, Just You" on Arbors Records.
He lives with his wife, the artist Sally Halverstadt, and their son, Nick, on Bleecker Street between Charles and Perry.

Musician Larry Ham grew up on a dairy farm in upstate Millbrook, a place where his family had roots stretching back three centuries. "My family is an old Dutch one that settled a farm there in the early 1700s," he says. "The schoolhouse that my wife and I bought and converted to our weekend getaway is where my dad, grandfather, and great-grandfather attended school."

Included in the farmhouse where Ham grew up was a Steinway piano that a great-great-great-aunt had bought in 1888. "Nobody ever played it much," he recalls. "But my mother decided that all of her children should have piano lessons. She's the musical side of our family, although she never had any training. As for Dad, he was a farmer. He didn't play an instrument and doesn't appear to be musical, but he certainly has an aesthetic nature. He loves the beauty of the natural world. And when he drove around the farm in the pickup truck he was always tuned into the classical station!"

So how did a farm boy with classical training wind up playing jazz piano? Particularly, as Ham says, "You didn't hear much jazz on a farm back in the 60s or early 70s!" It happened when he was finally living on his own. "One day someone gave me a John Coltrane recording and I just about fell over," he recalls. "Just trying to imagine the kind of human story that was being told through that music made me want to get closer to it. It was pretty much like the 'Saul on the Road to

Damascus' story: an instant conversion. So I bought a used piano and just started practicing. I found a teacher who told me to listen to this particular record, practice these chords, and I pretty much followed my sense that this was going to be my path in life."

After graduating college, Ham played around for a couple of years in the Catskills and on cruise ships, eventually moving to New York where he settled in Inwood. "That neighborhood was a little rough in the mid-eighties," he recalls. He met his wife at a party and after a while moved into her apartment on Bleecker Street and has lived there since 1990. For them, the Village was a great neighborhood to raise their son. "It's comfortable and quiet enough for that," Ham admits.

Addressing the kinds of changes he's seen in the West Village since moving here, Ham singles out the stores that now line his block. "We're right in the middle of a high-end clothing retail evolution here," he observes. "It used to be much more Mom and Pop, with a Laundromat on the corner and little stores that had been here for a long time. Now it's become very expensive commercial property. I think that makes it a little less unique. Of course, we're all unique. But there's something a little less singular about the character of the neighborhood. I sometimes walk down my street and wonder why they don't put a roof over it and call it a mall," he notes, laughing. "Then it would be all-weather!"

When asked what he thinks some of the biggest challenges are facing the West Village these days, Ham responds, "For me, the biggest issue is that there aren't many artists in the neighborhood anymore. It's just impossible for them to afford the properties and that's changed the character of things. So the challenge for the neighborhood is to rediscover and maintain that unique character that it has been noted for and to find ways to keep its identity."

He continues. "I've been on the board of my co-op almost since I moved here and it's really interesting the kinds of money now that come to buy apartments. People have piles of money now. That's something that my wife and I are grateful for in the sense that we've realized such an appreciation on our own investment. It's actually allowed us to borrow some money to fix up our place upstate. So you can't really complain. But there still is a certain nostalgia for when things were a little simpler and a little more neighborhood."

West Village Original • Music

Peter Leitch

March 2018

Photo: Chris Drukker

Jazz guitarist Peter Leitch was born in Canada in 1944. He released his first solo album in 1981 and about 15 more over the years. As a sideman, he has recorded with Jeri Brown, Oscar Peterson, Woody Shaw, and Pete Yellin, among others. In addition, he has worked as a journalist, photographer, and teacher. A few years ago, Leitch penned a memoir titled "Off the Books: A Jazz Life."

When Peter Leitch was old enough to start hanging out in Montreal clubs, it was at the same time that all the great jazz performers began coming through town. "It was the early 60s and their music was really the first thing I encountered in life that moved me in any way," he says. "I don't know why. But I do know I didn't have any motivation in any other direction until this music caught me like it did."

"I was given a guitar for a birthday present one year," he continues. "I had taken a few private lessons and learned the basics, but it wasn't really until I heard jazz that I pursued it. And I learned my craft right there on the bandstand. That's because there was a lot of work for local musicians in Montréal back then. Nightclubs were always hiring players. You also learned from the older musicians and they were actually generous with their time." What has the life of a jazz musician been like since then? "It's just like any other life; you go to work and you come home," Leitch says, laughing. "People think it's so great to see all these wonderful cities but when you're traveling as a working musician you don't get to be a tourist. You see the airport, train station, hotel, and the venue, but you don't get to see much else. I should say, though, that it was worth it because I was always moved by the music artistically."

A few years ago, after a successful career, Leitch suffered some health issues which left him unable to play guitar. Instead, he began concentrating on composing and arranging. "That really changed the way I look at music," he says. "I was an improvising instrumentalist for many years so I wasn't necessarily writing down a lot on paper. Writing is the opposite of creative improvisation. At the same time, I've come to believe the best jazz music is a mix of improvisation and written music. I think the goal of every jazz composer is to make it seamless so that the improvisation can sound written and the written can sound improvised."

Leitch also got very involved in photography for a period. "My ear was really developed from music and I wanted to bring my eye up to that level," he says. "I learned photography pretty much the same way I learned music—starting from nothing and trying to develop artistically. It's a good way to do it. You don't learn a lot of unnecessary things or just blindly learn a technical process. Instead, you have to keep striving to make more interesting music and more interesting photographs. I think that's the key to art: never stop trying to develop." Then he laughs. "No pun intended!"

Leitch and his wife, Sylvia, moved into West Village Houses on Greenwich Street in 1993. "This complex remains a legacy to Jane Jacobs," he says. "But there's a push by developers who think they can make a quick buck. They want to tear down these buildings and move us to another one. However, we love our home; we own our apartment and want to stay in it. It's just crazy what they're proposing. They couldn't pay me enough to move!"

In spite of the pressures that being in such a desirable area brings, Leitch thinks that one can still feel the sense of community and creative energy that was the old West Village. "It's just under the fabric of the new city," he says. "An example of this is a darkroom I used to rent in the basement of a building on Charles Street. It goes back to the 60s, still has the original equipment—like enlargers—and is still in use. So it's a link to when the Village was full of creative artists. That's the other thing: you never know who you're going to meet, particularly among the older residents of the Village. There are still some *very* interesting people here!"

West Village Original • Music

Denise Marsa

November 2019

Singer/songwriter Denise Marsa was born in Trenton, NJ in 1954. In addition to a decades-long career in the music business, Marsa owns Key Media Group, a public relations and marketing firm. She also mentors young singers and bands in navigating the industry. She recently wrote a one woman show about her life in music called "The Pass."

"I had good parents who were very affectionate and always encouraged me when I was growing up," says Denise Marsa. "Except when I told them I was moving to New York. Then they freaked out! But I was headstrong and said, 'I don't want to hear it. This is what I'm doing.' That was in the 70s when a lot of not so great stuff was going on here, so I don't blame them. But I was paying my own way, just like I had paid for my own education and I reassured them that I wouldn't be chewed up and spit out."

What drew Marsa to music in the first place? "I was always musical," she says. "My brother got a drum set for Christmas one year and I just started playing it. Same with the piano. I had both the instinct and the inclination. And my mother really pushed me. I think she had been overshadowed by her siblings growing up, so she put her energy into me. I was singing, taking acting classes and I landed my first professional gig in musical theater at age eight."

Fast forward all these years, and it was when Marsa was performing her songs in a couple of clubs that the idea for her current show came about. "My life has been funneled through song," she says. "There are people who are passionate about songwriting and I'm one of them. It's like breathing for us. When I did those club shows, people came up to me afterwards and said, 'Why aren't you a household name? You're like a female Billy Joel or Elton John.' Well, that's a long story. The story of my life, really! It's about timing and where you put your energy. It's about choice. Did I want to be rich and famous, or did I want to stay true to myself? It's a struggle to be an artist trying to stay relevant throughout it all. I've had a lot of luck but at the same time, things just happen out of your control. I'm sure part of it was me as well. There are so many things I said no to early in my career. But it doesn't matter now because I do what I do, and I still love doing it. My one-woman show is a vehicle to tell my story and get my songs heard. It's also where I started: in musical theatre. I've gone full circle."

These days, in addition to developing her show and running her PR company, Marsa is committed to mentoring young singers and bands. "When I was younger no one really empowered me to understand the music business, let alone the entertainment business," she says. "So instead of being angry, I decided to take my energy and put it towards helping young people protect themselves. I love doing it. There are a lot of dreamers in the music business but only a small percentage actually make a living in it. I think my experience can be instructive."

Marsa has lived in the same apartment on Christopher Street since she moved here over 40 years ago. How is the neighborhood different from those days? "Oh my God! How *isn't* it different?" she replies. "My perspective, though, is that New York both changes and doesn't change at the same time. By that I mean when you live in the West Village you get a chance to hold on to a bit more of the charm of life. And I think the most charming part of New York is the West Village, hands down. Everything is smaller, so maybe smaller is charming. But the people themselves live large lives in small spaces. I've done that as well."

"My apartment is full of history too," she continues. "It's small and dates from 1810, but I have a lot going on in that small space. My building has a back yard and it's been a very magical existence. I come into my house and shut everything off. Sometimes I wish I had one extra room. But this is what it is, and it's also a reminder to make the best of what you do have. That's always been my attitude: 'Make it work!'"

The High Line Park

It's a very special feeling here. I read an article recently in the New York Times that said the people in the West Village are the most satisfied in the city. Well, I'm one of them.

—Bob Gruen

West Village Original • Photography

Maggie Berkvist
December 2014

Photo: Alfie Timpson, 1970

Maggie Berkvist was born in Leicester, England. For over 50 years she was a photo editor and researcher, including a 20-year stint at the New York Times, after which she worked as a freelancer for publications such as LIFE. Since moving to New York City in November of 1954, she has spent most of those years happily living on Bank Street.

"I was the only child of an only child," photographer Maggie Berkvist says. "My father was an only child. My mother was adopted into a family when her mother died in childbirth. So I have no connections! I guess that's what made it easier for me to be footloose and fancy-free." This wanderlust led Berkvist to emigrate to Canada in 1952 with her first husband and then (minus said husband) to move to New York City two years later where she's been ever since.

It was while Berkvist was working at McCann Erickson that she found an opportunity to live on Bank Street. "I worked with a girl who was living there with her husband and always complaining about it," she says. "I asked her to let me know if she moved and, when she did, I got my basement room at number 315 for $35 a month. I was in heaven. I also got all the cockroaches you could count. And Peeping Toms! One fellow would creep down the steps and put his finger through the top of my window to try to raise the Venetian blinds and I would scream at him." She laughs. "I was five blocks from Louie's, a pub on Sheridan Square, and I was exploring New York with friends. This was how my life settled into the West Village in 1956."

That same year Berkvist began her career at the *New York Times*. "They really gave me my education and my opportunity," she says. "They knew I was into photography and they felt I had potential. When one woman left the picture desk for maternity leave, they gave me a chance. Well, she never came back and I was there for 23 years!" Did she enjoy the job? "I thought I'd died and gone to heaven," she admits. "I loved what I did and the people I was working with. I remember a friend of ours was doing a job-related questionnaire in which she asked us to name our ten favorite things. Afterwards, she said to me, 'You're the only person who's ever said that work was one of them!'"

After a second marriage where she lived in Brooklyn Heights and the Upper West Side, Berkvist returned (minus that husband) to Bank Street in 1965. "Back then, there wasn't a 'West Village,'" she says. "There was just Greenwich Village. Writers, actors, artists, and students came here because it was cheap and bohemian. And it still had a very political edge." When asked what major differences she sees today, Berkvist considers for a moment. "I tell you what's interesting," she finally says. "For any struggling youngster to imagine they can come and live in the Village today, forget it! Once the real estate guys came romping in, the area became out of most people's league. This place has nothing to do with the West Village, as we knew it in the 50s, 60s, 70s, and even the 80s, when they started to trickle in. Remember the yuppies? That was the beginning of the end."

Yet, Berkvist admits that if you look carefully you can still find pockets of compatible souls. "I'm so glad I'm here and that I found a little corner where there is this remainder of the Village of yore," she says. "One of the great moments of discovery for me was during Hurricane Sandy. My little watering hole—the Left Bank—managed to stay open all those nights with just candlelight. We were all hanging out like the good old days, talking to one another and giving each other tips on how to survive until the electricity came back on."

And after celebrating the "remarkable milestone" of six decades here, Berkvist has to admit that most of it was due to luck. "I really was incredibly lucky and it's all to do with being in the right place at the right time," she enthuses. "It's amazing! I look back now because I'm so old and I think how lucky I've been in my life, over and over again. It wasn't that I had the education or the connections, either. It's just that New York and the West Village was really where I was meant to be."

West Village Original • Photography

Bob Gruen

April 2009

Photo: H. Toreson

Rock-and-roll photographer Bob Gruen has worked closely with major attractions such as John Lennon & Yoko Ono, Tina Turner, The Rolling Stones, Led Zeppelin, Elton John, and Kiss. A Greenwich Village resident since 1965, he settled into the newly created Westbeth complex in 1970 and still lives there with his wife, Elizabeth.

It took a couple of failed attempts at college to get photographer Bob Gruen to move to New York. It was at the third school he tried, in Baltimore, where his sociology professor told him one day that he should be living in Greenwich Village. "So I moved to Sullivan Street in June of 1965," he recalls. "I showed up at my friend's apartment with my cartons and it turned out that the Feast of St. Anthony was going on right outside our door. The first ten days I was here we didn't cook anything. We just ran down to the street and got our food."

Growing up on Long Island, it seems as if there never was a time when Gruen couldn't remember being around a camera or the darkroom. "My mother and father were both attorneys," he says. "But my mom photographed as a hobby and taught herself how to develop and print as well. When I was very little she started to take me in the darkroom with her. I used to count the seconds while we were developing the prints. When I was eight years old I got my first camera, a Brownie, and I got my first 35mm camera for my bar mitzvah."

Before Gruen started photographing rock bands, there wasn't a field called "Rock-and-Roll Photography." "I'm one of the people who invented it", Gruen says. "I was alive when rock–and-roll started, I liked the music, and I liked photography so it all came together. After I moved to the Village I ended up living with a rock-and-roll band and taking pictures of them. When they finally got a record deal, their company used my photos for the album. After that, it kind of snowballed."

One of his most famous associations was with John Lennon and Yoko Ono. "In 1972 I was asked to take pictures for an interview in *After Dark* magazine," he recalls. "The story was actually about Elephant's Memory, a downtown band who were backing up John Lennon in the recording studio. I took the pictures with the band and then I suggested that John and Yoko join them for some as well. John and Yoko liked those pictures when they saw them and invited me to spend more time with them. Since I lived in Westbeth and they were on Bank Street at that time, it was very convenient for us to see each other and that's how our friendship started."

How different was the far west Village in the early 70s? "When I first moved into this part of the Village it was deserted," Gruen laughs. "It seemed like miles from anywhere that people were. You had to go up to Eighth Avenue to get a taxi. There was even a little pony farm at Washington and Tenth Streets! They would rent out the ponies for birthdays. Within the next few years they took down a lot of the older buildings here and built those low-rise brick buildings along Washington Street." As for the waterfront, in those days it was all dilapidated old piers. "The pier here on Bank Street in the summertime was like a beach," he recalls. "There could be thousands of sunbathers on a weekend afternoon, with people selling ice cream and beer. Over the years the piers kept catching on fire so the city cut off access to them. Much later they ended up finally taking them down."

He knew things were changing, though, when about ten years ago he was able to get a cab on Washington Street. "I thought, 'Wow, the neighborhood is picking up!' That's because the Meat Packing district started developing as a destination. The biggest changes that I've seen are the increase in the rents and the increase in the population. A lot of that is due to the Hudson River Park. It's a lot better than I expected it to be and it made it possible for other people to want to live here."

Does Gruen still enjoy living in the West Village? "Oh, yeah, very much," he says. "It's a very special feeling. The fact that's it a little crooked compared to the rest of New York is part of it. It actually feels like a village. At the same time there's a lot of creative people here and they tend to have a live and let live attitude. I read an article recently in the *New York Time*s that said the people in the West Village are the most satisfied in the city. Well, I'm one of them."

West Village Original • Photography

Rose Hartman
November 2011

Photo: Marsin Digital

New York-born photographer Rose Hartman's work has been featured in a number of solo books, including "Birds of Paradise," "Incomparable Women of Style," and "Incomparable Couples." Her work has also appeared in countless publications and she recently donated her archives to the library at FIT. Visit her at www.rosehartman.com.

For photographer Rose Hartman, it turned out that a hobby of her father's would leave a lasting impression. "While my father was a jewelry designer by trade, his hobby was taking pictures," she recalls. "In fact, most of the photos I have of my family were taken by him. So I think photography was inculcated in me at an early age. I always saw my father with a camera, and I loved him very much."

Hartman was born on East 9th Street and Avenue C, raised in Queens and went on to major in English at CCNY. It was while teaching at the then very rough Seward Park High School on Delancey Street that she decided to change careers. "As much as I enjoyed teaching, I detested babysitting students," she says. "I was very frustrated, and my boyfriend kept asking me, 'What would you enjoy doing?' I remember saying I would love to take photographs. So I went to a summer workshop at Sun Valley and there I was lucky enough to photograph the wedding of Joan Hemingway, Ernest's granddaughter. I got the front cover of the *Daily News Record* and it was a big deal. I got paid, too! So I had found a passion."

Pursuing this passion, Hartman left teaching and went on to chronicle the world of beauty, celebrity and style for more than three decades. One of her favorite haunts was Studio 54 during its heyday. "It was the most fantastic club I've ever been to," Hartman says. "I didn't go all the time but just enough so that I could mingle and shoot my pictures." One of these—her photo of Bianca Jagger on a white horse in the club itself—remains an iconic image of that era. Hartman also debunks the myth that her photos were elaborately posed. "They were not," she says. "There would be a huge crowd of people and I would have to pull out my subject and create an intimate moment. But it was never really intimate. It was a creation. And a lot of people who've seen my work don't believe that. They think I set up my scenarios. But Bianca, who was very beautiful, was on that horse for about one minute before they took her off and led the horse out. I had to act quickly but that photo is the one that defines me."

What was Hartman's attraction to the glitter of the jet set? "Well, as a child we walked up six flights of stairs to our apartment," she says drily. "We'll start with that. It was also an entrance into a world that was unlike mine. This was a world of billionaires who traveled effortlessly. And I was very attracted to that." Yet her access to these people did not necessarily translate into friendships. "A lot of the people would be very friendly when I was photographing them, but it never went further," she says. "So I think that many of my experiences were during the 'allotted time,' one might say. In a way, I was providing a service and I have to say I performed unstintingly. I made everyone look gorgeous."

As a resident of Charles Street since 1963, Hartman has had a front row seat to major change. "The small, local businesses have all been tossed out and the millionaire designers took over each and every shop," she say. "Marc Jacobs, of course, is the leader of the pack. I said to him, 'Marc, you know you have changed the neighborhood.' And he said, 'In a good or bad way?' I couldn't believe he actually asked that! Thanks to these shops, it's almost impossible to walk on the streets of my neighborhood because it's so crowded. People now shop instead of going to a gallery or looking at the architecture. They're not involved in the historic nature of this fantastic locale. I could say the history of the Village is of no interest to these visitors. Of course that's a generalization, but I think it's a fair one."

Does this mean she's lost her affection for the neighborhood? "Are you kidding?," she replies. "If it's a gorgeous late afternoon I will get on my bicycle, ride along the Hudson, watch the sunset and think, 'My God, this is the most beautiful visual that I can have.' I still love it here!"

West Village Original • Photography

David Plakke

May 2016

Photographer David Plakke, born in Michigan in 1951, has been a resident of Westbeth for 22 years. Plakke has photographed architecture, fine art, cultural events, musicians, artists, and the corporate world. He has had two books of photographs published and has an ongoing photographic and video project called "Tribes." Visit him at www.davidplakke.com.

As the adopted child of an extremely religious Calvinist Dutch couple in Michigan, photographer David Plakke was always yearning to break free of their constraints. "Truthfully, from a young age I realized I was from a very different lineage," he says. "And yet, interestingly enough, I ended up focusing on two things my Dad was very much into as well: music and photography."

With his parents and his sister, Plakke would perform at fairs and homes for seniors. "My mother played accordion, my Dad clarinet and saxophone, my sister piano, and I alto sax," he says. "We would play everything from 'Sentimental Journey' to 'Amazing Grace.'" And by the time Plakke was eight years old he had a Brownie camera. "As a kid I even built my own enlarger—a box and a couple of pieces of glass," he recalls. "I would just make contact prints. So it was music—now the guitar—and photography all through school. When I was drafted into the Army during the Vietnam fiasco, I spent the whole time taking pictures and going into the darkroom. It was one of the ways I kept my sanity."

When he finally had to choose between a career as a musician or a photographer, how did he? "I thought I could always do music but I'm really not into poverty," Plakke says. "I've always had a practical side and it seemed I could make more money in photography. Now my work allows me a lifestyle that I love."

According to Plakke, being a photographer isn't just about technical skill but having the personality for it as well. "You have to be charming," he says, laughing. "You really do! You can have beautiful equipment and an education from SVA or Parsons, but if you don't have the personality you're going to be nothing more than a good technician. Especially when shooting people. You have to gain their confidence. You're going to make them look better than they think they ever could and when that happens everybody's happy. The technique is not rocket science and with digital it's becoming easier and easier to be a photographer. But the thing that people don't get is how important personality is."

In addition to having the requisite personality, Plakke also likes the fact that there's no shelf life to his career as long as he stays healthy. "That's the cool thing about being this age," he admits. "I can still take pictures. Of course, I'd still like to be 21. But until I can't pick the camera up any more—it weighs ten pounds—I just keep getting better. It's not like being a singer and losing your voice. As a photographer, until your sight goes or your strength goes, it just keeps going. It's a great thing."

Plakke moved to New York in 1984 after finishing graduate school and lived in various places. When the Westbeth office called in 1995 he was sharing a 7,500 square foot loft with 18-foot ceilings in Hoboken. "I had a huge dark room and it was a photographer's paradise," he says. "Then I moved into a 450 square foot space here. What a difference! But it was the best thing to happen to me. Westbeth is like the jewel of New York. There are some goofy people here but a lot of cool people as well. And they basically like to be left alone like I do. I love the West Village. Where else would you want to live in this city?"

Aside from the obvious, has the neighborhood changed much since he first moved in? "When I first moved here I would come home at three in the morning and there would be transvestite hookers standing on the corner," Plakke says. "Beautiful, seven foot guys in high heels and short skirts. And they would say, 'Hey baby, how you doing? Are you lonely yet?' They're gone now. Where did they go? I don't know. Now I come home at three in the morning and it's screaming drunk people from New Jersey." He laughs. "It just ain't the same!"

West Village Original • Photography

Suzanne Poli
June 2020

Photo: Suzanne Poli

Photographer Suzanne Poli was born in Gowanus, Brooklyn. Poli's photographs are represented in the collections of numerous institutions and have appeared in film and on television. Her image "Nightsticks" opens the classic black-and-white American Experience PBS documentary "Stonewall Uprising." Poli has lived on Christopher Street for over fifty years.

"I've photographed ever since I was little," says photographer Suzanne Poli. "I took the family pictures for birthdays and holidays. All of the ones we have, in fact. Then I began to paint and I loved it. I was really good at it. But I started to use the camera as a means for recording my daily life. It was very exciting and gradually I stopped painting and began photographing every day." Suzanne's parents tried to nudge her along a different path, however. "There was always dialog about how I should be a secretary and this other kind of person, not the one I was," she says. "So they were surprised when 'this other person' found a voice. They knew I was talented but they discouraged me by saying 'You have stars in your eyes' or 'You can't do that.' The push and pull of it all was tough."

The irony is that Poli definitely thinks she got her artistic bent from her parents. "My father was very sweet, gentle, and kind," she says. "There was a cultured quality about him that I really admired. He was elegant even though the work he did was bad for his health. My mother was very feisty, vivacious, and descriptive. She had a dark side as well from a life that hadn't been easy. This is where I got a lot of my talent from."

To support herself, for many years Poli worked as a waitress in a Village restaurant called Kenneret. "I didn't particularly like it. It was really hard. No wonder I made sure my daughter got an Ivy League education," she says, laughing. "But through all of that I had my own dark room and studio, which was my passion and kept me alive and connected. I can only thrive if I have a special place. It would have been better if I had gone to school, but I didn't have the support structure. It would have given me more confidence to take things for myself. But the journey has been worth it. My life was so full and rich anyway." As for the "artistic moment," Poli claims the best one is when she's creating the image. "That moment is a very spiritual place to be. It's a place that keeps evolving, a very soothing and healing place. It's often said that my images are very thick with feeling. I work really hard on an image. I'm composing and crafting it as I look through the viewfinder. I like to say that's a moment when I'm actually focused."

Since the very first Gay Pride parade 50 years ago, Poli has been photographing it, both from her window and on the street. "I feel when I'm photographing that I'm actually moving a cause forward and creating the change that is happening," she says. "Christopher Street was always a place for protest and the march started as a protest against ill treatment. In a way, I feel I helped create the movement. I was very involved with gay rights because I thought that everybody should have the right to be who they are. I was also deeply involved with the AIDS movement. But whether the fight is about race, gender, or sexual preference I have to support it because this is who I am. I live for social causes and have very strong political feelings."

Having lived on Christopher Street for over five decades, Poli has seen her share of changes. "It was very special and different when I first lived here," she says. "There were wonderful, individual shops on the street. I suppose all the fancy haute couture shops that eventually moved in made it 'nice' in that everything got gentrified and cleaned up. It made the neighborhood more upscale, but the change is pretty drastic. I don't know where it's going but I'm sure it will always sustain itself in some way. It will always be a special place. It's still lovely and even today there's a very thick palette of passion here. When people come to the West Village they have a different way of treating the neighborhood. They have a certain kind of respect for it and find it very special."

West Village Original • Photography

Nancy Rudolph

May 2010

Nancy Rudolph began photographing in the late 1940's while working in Europe through the Marshall Plan. Her first photographic essay appeared in the New York Times Magazine in the 1950's. Throughout her career she has had seventeen solo exhibits and has published three books of her photos. Ms. Rudolph moved to the Village in 1952, and has lived in the same house on West 11th Street since 1956.

After a few unsuccessful attempts at college as a young woman, Nancy Rudolph's mother suggested she take up shorthand and typing. It was a suggestion that would turn out to have far-reaching consequences. "My mother said I could go anywhere and get any kind of job with those skills," Rudolph recalls. "So I went to Sadie Brown's Collegiate Secretarial School in the Grand Central Building. I must have had ten jobs in one year! I was not cut out for that kind of work."

Eventually, Rudolph went to Europe and was living in Paris where she applied for a job through the Marshall Plan. "There were a lot of Americans in Paris those days, both on the GI Bill and working for the government," she says. "I applied at the ECA (Bureau of Educational and Cultural Affairs) and ended up working in Rome for a couple of years as a secretary doing—of all things—shorthand and typing. As pleased as my mother was with that, she was very upset that I overstayed my time in Europe and I wasn't at home getting married!" Rudolph laughs. "But I had a wonderful life there. I finally did come home, met Alan Rudolph, and married him."

While Rudolph subsequently "liberated" herself after twenty-five years of marriage to her husband, the photography she began doing while overseas remained a constant in her life. "I started as a painter," she relates. "When I went to Europe, I brought my paints, easel, and an old camera that belonged in the family. And when I was in Rome,

I took a trip with a friend to Berlin. This was during the time of the airlift. We stayed with an army officer and his family so I went to the PX and bought myself a decent camera. The first real photographs I took were of people digging out of war-torn Berlin. That was 1949."

Why did photography become her means of expression? "I always wanted to say things about the human condition," Rudolph explains. "I have a big social conscience and I wanted to spotlight issues that I thought should be examined and understood and, if necessary, changed. That was the real motivation of my photography. I couldn't do that through painting so that's why I picked up a camera. I understood a lot more through photographs." This approach to the medium also informed her philosophy of it as well. "I never looked at photography as an art," she says. "I looked at it as a way to say something about the world."

A resident of the Village since the 50s, Rudolph claims this is the only place she wanted to live in New York. "I've never lived in any other part of the city," she says. "My husband wanted to move to the suburbs because he grew up in New York. And I grew up in the suburbs on Long Island and vowed never to go back!" With such longevity, it's no surprise that Rudolph's strongest desire is "to preserve as much of the Village as can be preserved." "I was involved with the whole Jefferson Market Courthouse fight when they were trying to tear it down," she says. "I was also very involved in Washington Square Park when they were going to put Fifth Avenue right through it. I think that was the first victory that citizens had over an issue like that."

While Rudolph's love affair with Greenwich Village continues to this day, it is difficult at times to reconcile the past with the present. One of the biggest changes for her is the growth of both NYU and the New School in her neighborhood. "The New School has never been very invasive, but now it is," she says. "I think it's awful. And then I say to my son, 'I think it's terrible!' like an old codger. But my son replies that these people are being educated to go into the world and make a difference. So how can you argue against that?"

West Village Original • Photography

Jan Staller
January 2012

Photo: Mark Seliger

Long Island-born photographer Jan Staller has been in New York City since 1976 and a homeowner on Charles Street since 1993. In addition to numerous editorial assignments, solo shows, and group shows, he has had two monographs of his enigmatic photographs published: "Frontier New York" and "On Planet Earth." His work is in the collections of numerous public and private institutions.

When photographer Jan Staller first moved to New York in 1976, it was his living arrangements that would ultimately influence his early photography. "I lived in a very dark loft with no direct light on Walker Street," he recalls. "As a result, I was drawn to the river for a sense of nature. I would end up on the abandoned West Side Highway and it was a great refuge. When they started to demolish it I thought maybe I'd better take some photographs. In a way, that was my pursuit of nature along the Hudson. Actually, it *is* nature. It's the river, and sunlight, and the horizon. It's not the experience you get anywhere else but at the fringe of the city."

"My early photographs were made at twilight," he continues. "That was for two reasons. One was that I would always go out at the end of the day because I just wanted to enjoy the last hour of daylight and the sunset. Then I found myself staying out later and later and watching the street lights come on. This twilight effect was very dramatic because as the lights came on and the sky drew darker the street would become brighter. It was a cinematic quality almost like stage lighting and it was wonderful. I was able to take some very mysterious and ethereal photographs."

Many of these photographs of the West Side Highway ended up in a monograph entitled *Frontier New York*, published by Hudson Hills Press in 1988. These images represented what Staller likes best about photography, "It's the sense of discovery," he says. He goes on to explain that one of the first things people did with photography was to bring back images of faraway lands or ancient ruins. They went exploring. "When I began to work," he continues, "there was this question I posed to myself: Could I 'explore' the world without going anywhere and just work close to home? So I did, and it was a kind of discovery. To visit a location once or twice gives you the lay of the land. But to visit it again and again—as I did with the West Side Highway—is very valuable. In the hands, mind, and eye of a practitioner, photographs can show us something different from what we might perceive if we were there ourselves. I wanted others to be able to see the place as I saw it."

Since buying a house on Charles Street two decades ago, Staller has witnessed first-hand the changes to the West Village. "It's become much more dense with high rises," he says. "And there's actually more noise in the neighborhood because the old brick buildings that blocked the sound from the highway were torn down in 2000 for the Meier towers. But I certainly am impressed with the personalities that have moved into the neighborhood. I have some very distinguished neighbors and I'm sure a lot of them got here through their hard work." And Staller can't imagine living anywhere else now. "It's my penultimate resting place," he says. "It's not about the exploration and mystery that it had in the 1970s when it was still dingy piers blocking the river, but Hudson River Park is a wonderful resource now just to appreciate on an aesthetic basis."

Staller returns to his early years of exploring the West Side Highway and how it had the sense of a frontier back then. "Because of that," he says, "one could experience the same kinds of feelings that one could get in the woods: solitude and peace. That was a quality I enjoyed for quite a while until they tore it all down. Of course the river and the light are still there, but the experience is very different. I certainly wouldn't claim any part of New York for myself, but I certainly enjoyed it by myself for the few years that it was there. Walking up on the Highway on a snowy day, my footprints would be the only ones. That you could find this kind of solitude in a city of eight million was kind of remarkable."

West Village Original • Photography

SuZen
May 2016

Photo: Lucienne Weinberger

Photographer SuZen, who moved into Westbeth in 1971, was born and raised in Brooklyn. Her artwork has grown from traditional black-and-white print images shown in galleries to large-scale performances in public spaces. Retired from teaching photography, her newest multi-media installation is called "Transmigration," inspired by Buddha's teachings.

Coming from a family in which no one was an artist or even interested in art, the photographer SuZen claims that she was the black sheep of a family of four. "I think I was one of those lost psychos," she says, laughing. "I ended up in a family I didn't belong in. Ever since I was very young I was drawing. When I was five, I drew a mural on our living room wall. Of course I denied it and my Mom didn't really believe I did it anyway because it was so good! But I was usually off doing my own thing. Growing up, I really couldn't wait to leave the home."

While she had always taken drawing classes—first at the Brooklyn Library and then at the Brooklyn Museum—SuZen didn't discover photography until she was a student at American University. "It was a fluke," she says. "I was a sophomore when this dorm mate asked me if she could photograph me. As a result, I became intrigued with photography and I immediately fell in love with working in the dark room. There's something kind of magical about it: when you're in the flow and you get lost into your art and there's no time, just you into what you're doing. To me, that is the most wonderful state to be in."

Photography also helped SuZen feel more connected with the world. "I was always extremely shy and having the camera enabled me to go in and out of places and feel like I was a part of them," she says. "Always as the observer, though, and the outsider. But as artists that is what we do, isn't it? We observe. Especially when I'm holding a camera up to my eye. A camera sees everything so I get to select a point of view and decide what to photograph. On that level photography is very wonderful. I always loved—and still do—taking photographs in the outside world but then being alone with them and creating the art."

SuZen was always one of those artists who would do the work and then "forget about it." Now that she has a 50-year retrospective, she's seeing things in a different light. "I'm noticing how my images really do connect, after all," she says. "What has changed is that my process is almost totally digital now. I use Photoshop to manipulate my images and it does open up different possibilities for my creations." And while she doesn't work in the dark room these days, she still has one. She was going to give it up a few years ago but just couldn't do it. "I think one day I will go back," she says. "There's something wonderful about being in a room with orange lights and running water. It's like being back in the womb and totally safe."

SuZen moved into WestBeth in 1971 and after a few sublets finally got her own apartment there. "I can hardly believe it's been 45 years," she says. "This area was very scary back then, basically truckers and prostitutes. I parked my car for $13 a month under the elevated West Side Highway. Of course my windows got smashed and my tires got slashed, but the price was right!" She laughs. "Now I've literally watched this neighborhood transform in front of my eyes. A new building blocks my sunset views and another one my Empire State Building view. I'm not crazy about all this change but it has been interesting to watch. A lot of the character of the Village has been lost but I feel blessed to have been a part of its older self and to have had the experience of it."

And despite the changes around her, SuZen has always gone with life's flow and still follows that path. "Never in my life did I know what I was doing next," she says. "I'm always open and allowing synchronicity to guide me. By that I mean being open to what life would bring to me instead of having clarity about where I'm going. It boils down to trusting that the universe will guide me to what is next in my life."

West Village Original • Poetry

Edward Field

February 2011

Photo: Neil Derrick

Poet and author Edward Field was born in Brooklyn in 1924. His books of poetry include "Magic Words: Poems," "Counting Myself Lucky," and "Stand Up, Friend, with Me," which won the 1962 Lamont Poetry Prize. Under the pseudonym of Bruce Elliot, Field has also collaborated on several popular novels with his life partner of fifty years, Neil Derrick, with whom he shares a home in Westbeth.

It was while on a three-day train trip in basic training during WWII that poet Edward Field discovered his life's work and joy. "I was in the Army Air Corps and a Red Cross worker gave me a paperback," he recalls. "It was an anthology of great poems. I read it the entire trip and when I got off the train I knew I was going to be a poet. I had never known what I wanted to be before. I couldn't imagine what to do with my life but when I read that book I knew: 'Poetry!'"

"Later on I was stationed in England," he continues. "While in the Officers' Club one night I met a poet, an officer. He told me about all these other poets he knew in London and I started reading modern poetry. I discovered there was a whole world of living poets out there as well."

After his war service, Field attended NYU on the GI Bill but dropped out after two years. "I headed for the Left Bank in Paris," he says. "It seemed the nicest place to go at the time, the most stimulating and friendly to budding poets. It was much easier as a gay man as well. I spent a year in Europe, but it was very hard to get work and I had no money so I came back to the States."

The ensuing decade here turned out to be a struggle as well. "The 50s were a very difficult time in America," Field says. "I think being a Lefty made it hard because you felt you were against where America was going. I wasn't a member of the Communist Party, but it was still very hard to get a job because I couldn't do anything. So I had a lot of little jobs and I kept writing. Of course I was crazy from the war as well. I think if you go into combat you don't come out of it unscathed. I was in a lot of therapy in the fifties. Then I met my partner, Neil, and that's what really saved my life."

It was in 1962 that Field had his big break professionally. "My manuscript for a book of poems was rejected 25 times before it won the Lamont Award," he says. "Then Grove Press published it as *Stand Up, Friend, With Me*. It received excellent reviews and it changed my life. It was wonderful to finally find my work. I also was able to travel the country giving poetry readings and I earned a living doing it."

For Field, being in the West Village for many decades means that the past is constantly present. "When I walk through the Village, I really walk down a memory lane," he says. "I know what the old shops were before Marc Jacobs moved in. I hear the sounds of the old Village. There used to be typewriters clacking from windows as writers wrote their novels. There were violinists practicing, sopranos trilling away, and guys walking around with paint-covered Levis. It's all here in my memory and consequently very real."

However, Field acknowledges that it's a world that has changed utterly in every way except externally. "The buildings are still the same ones that have always been here," he says. "But everything else has changed due to economics. Fortunately, when the Village went upscale, Westbeth was here for us artists to move into. It was a way to keep us here. We're the survivors, the last of the artists in the Village."

When asked if he has any hopes for the future of the West Village, Field candidly admits, "Well, I won't be here that much longer." Then he thinks for a moment. "But if a place like Westbeth can survive," he continues, "it will be good for keeping alive the memory of what the Village was: a safety valve for all of America where people fled to so they could create art and express their sexuality. In every sense it was a whole radical world when the rest of the country was devoted to business, respectability, and morality. The Village was the place of ideas."

West Village Original • Poetry

George Held

June 2012

Photo: Maggie Berkvist

George Held–born in White Plains, NY–has published fifteen volumes of poetry, including a trilogy of chapbooks on nature themes. His work has been read by Garrison Keillor on NPR's "The Writer's Almanac." A graduate of Brown, with a Ph.D. from Rutgers, he was a Fulbright lecturer and is a former longtime professor at Queens College, CUNY.

"I love the Village," writer and longtime resident George Held admits. "I think it's still a great place for a writer. There's a sense of creativity going on all around. I love the literary history and I know where all the great writers lived. In fact, when I first moved here, Marianne Moore and I banked at the same place on Sixth Avenue!"

Growing up in Westchester, Held had his parents to thank for opening up the world of literature to him. "My parents read a lot themselves and they read to me when I was little," he recalls. "I think they made me very partial to the printed word and I was a good student in English throughout school. I ended up majoring in English in college. My parents had a pretty good library as well, with a lot of books that became classics. They seemed to have an eye for buying a new book that was later regarded as having some substance."

How did Held become a writer? "Well, I started out as a kind of academic writer doing literary criticism and I always found that a mixed blessing," he says. "I enjoyed the research, less the writing, and even less trying to get those essays published!" In the early 80s, Held developed a condition called Chronic Fatigue Syndrome and took a sabbatical during which time he was supposed to do academic writing but wasn't feeling well enough to do it. "I started to write poetry because I thought it took less concentrated energy," he says, laughing. "I started to send them around and getting them accepted. I was encouraged and I've continued to write creatively—poetry, fiction, translations, and books reviews—ever since. But I'm especially fond of poetry."

"I really love to write," Held continues. "I've always had a lively imagination. What usually happens is that I will think of, remember, or see something that creates images in my mind. Then the words come next. In the last few years I've been trying to write poetry that's more spare than in the past. I write a lot of Haiku and teach it at workshops. I like to use word play and wit and I think that is also more conducive to a shorter form."

Held moved into the West Village in 1967. "I came with my PhD in hand and my job at Queens College starting in the fall of that year," he says. A year later he worked on Norman Mailer's mayoral campaign. "Mailer was a Village habitué," Held says. "You'd see him in bars and at the *Village Voice* office. There used to be a bowling alley above Sheridan Square and that's where I folded envelopes for his campaign. He and Jimmy Breslin were running as Mayor and Lieutenant Mayor. Their slogan was 'Throw the rascals out!'"

Held says there's no two ways about the fact that the Village has gone way upscale since his arrival. "The people you see on the street in the morning going to work are well dressed and carrying briefcases now. When I first came here, people wore casual dress and they didn't look very prosperous. They were here because the rents were affordable. Now it's exactly the opposite. I suppose it's just the way of the world. I know people love to gripe about it but I don't see what we who love the old Village can do to keep our fingers in the dike."

For now, it's an unusual arrangement that Held has with his wife that enables them to stay here. "My wife lives in a co-op a block away from me," he says. "That's because we kept our apartments when we married. We met in 1978 and married in 2002! We've known each other all those years and we just stayed put. We both love the Village and we feel the best way to enjoy it, and afford it, is to keep our own respective apartments." There are perks to this arrangement as well. "I must say it's the envy of a large number of our married friends," he says, laughing heartily.

I've seen a lot of changes. When I walk through the neighborhood it's almost like I see in 3D. I see the building that was there before and the one before that.

—Dina Paisner

Cherry Lane Theatre

West Village Original • Theatre

Charles Busch

July 2010

Actor, playwright, novelist, screenwriter, and gender-illusionist Charles Busch's first hit, "Vampire Lesbians of Sodom," opened in 1985 at the Provincetown Playhouse and ran for five years. Since then he has written such plays as "The Lady in Question," "Red Scare on Sunset," "The Tale of the Allergist's Wife," and "The Divine Sister," co-wrote the musical "Swingtime Canteen," and wrote the screenplay for "Psycho Beach Party."

"I'm a true New Yorker, born in Mt. Sinai Hospital," says writer and actor Charles Busch. "When I was born we were living in the Fleetwood section of The Bronx. Then we moved to Hartsdale in Westchester and I lived there until I was about 12. At that point my Aunt Lillian adopted me and took me to live with her in Murray Hill."

It turned out Busch's Aunt Lillian was a woman of great insight. "She totally got who I was, what my strengths were," he reminisces. "Parents often have a fantasy of what they want their children to be but with my aunt, I think no matter what my interests were, she would've done everything she could to cultivate them. She took great pleasure in helping me pursue theatre, writing, acting, and even drawing. She sent me to every kind of class. I really had everything going for me."

Busch attended the High School of Music and Art in the City and then left for Chicago to attend Northwestern University. It was there that he realized his career path was not going to be what he thought it might. "My assumption was that I was going to have a career just as an actor for hire," he says. "But I was never cast in a play at Northwestern. I started to see that I was this eccentric type and if I wasn't being cast in university theatre it would probably be even harder professionally." At the same time, while back in New York on school breaks, Busch started seeing more experimental theatre. "That was the golden age for it," Busch says. "I would see productions of The Performance Group,

Jeff Weiss and, above all, Charles Ludlam. It was Ludlam who really opened my eyes to the fact that the theatrical experience could be whatever I chose it to be and that I could write roles for myself."

Busch began doing just that, establishing a reputation for sending up and celebrating classic film genres. While the trajectory of his career took him from small dives all the way to Broadway, he holds a special place in his heart for the struggling early days. "I must say I've always had kind of a taste for the raffish," he confesses. "It never seemed to me a terrible thing to produce a play on a shoestring in a horrible dive. Maybe because I come from such a bourgeois upbringing, but I just adored being involved—at least part time—in a kind of decadent netherworld. I reveled in it. I loved it and I miss it."

Busch moved into the West Village in 1978 when he found a place on 12th Street. "I was the youngest person in my building," he says. "Otherwise, it was just old, eccentric Village characters. There was the octogenarian Swiss yoga teacher. There was the little old Italian lady, dressed all in black, who paid about $10 a month in rent. There was the strange, elderly communist activist who had a big map of the world on her wall. Finally, we had a marvelous old female impersonator whose apartment was right out of *La Cage Aux Folles*. Eventually they all died off and by the time I left the building, I was sort of the old female impersonator!" He laughs. "It's inevitable!"

Busch is currently ensconced on Bank Street and claims he loves it so much that it makes him a little bit reclusive. "I never want to leave this block," he admits. "This is my home here and I just love it. I think the West Village has the greatest charm of any area in New York." Part of that charm is thanks to the beautiful renovations to some of the local parks. "Abingdon Square is like an MGM musical," he observes. "And Jackson Square is right out of *The Bandwagon*."

Yet even such sylvan surroundings can't prevent the occasional lament about the pace of change in the neighborhood. "I was complaining recently to a friend," Busch admits. "I was going on about how Bleecker Street is now just all designer clothing shops and my friend said, 'Oh, boo-hoo! I feel SO sorry for you!'" Busch laughs heartily at himself, saying, "My friend is right. That's a small price to pay to live in heaven."

West Village Original • Theatre

Peter Carlaftes

August 2015

Photo: Matthew Murphy

Writer and performer Peter Carlaftes was born and raised in the Bronx. He has published works in all genres: playwriting (including the spoof "Spin-Dry"), comic writing (the recent "A Year on Facebook"), and collections of poetry (including "Drunkyard Dog"). In addition, he and his partner, Kat Georges, own and run Three Rooms Press, a leading independent publisher of "cut-the-edge" creative writing.

Growing up in the Bronx after his parents divorced, writer Peter Carlaftes did a lot of bouncing around. "I lived with all my relatives and was all over the place," he says. "It's not much of a tale, though. I enjoyed my handball and the streets, but the Bronx never really appealed to me. I always came down to the city and a lot of times I'd wind up in the West Village. I was always looking up so much I'm surprised no one cut my throat!" He laughs. "My upbringing certainly affected me as a person, but it's nothing I haven't dealt with and put into perspective."

Besides, Carlaftes found that he could take care of himself. "Even though the particulars of my life weren't secure, I always had a sense of security inside myself," he says. "I'm also mostly self-educated and I was a good student as far as that goes. I did a lot of work on my own. Mostly I was just huffing around trying to figure out a way to make my dream come true, which was to be a writer."

How did he make that happen? "I started out writing back in the 70s," he replies. "I wrote a lot of short stories about crazy things in my life, kind of like Charles Bukowski but in my own voice, of course. It wasn't until the 90s when I was out in San Francisco that I got involved in writing plays. In doing so I ran into my partner, Kat. She had a theatre and we turned that into a den of creativity for ten years. It was a great experience, making sure the audience had a place to get away to and be inside of another creation. There's a day-to-day horror that most people get swept up by and art is definitely a way out of that."

At the same time, the couple began Three Rooms Press when they started stapling chapbooks together with their own and other people's poetry. Over twenty years later, Carlaftes claims there's a certain brand that the Press is known for. "There's a key component that I can't really describe," he says. "It's always different from the other stuff but it's still going to shine. I do know it's got to be something that inspires. That's a necessity. If you can't be somewhat open in art there's not much room to go forward. I have no judgments on anyone else's process, but for me that's the criteria." In fact, this is key to Carlaftes' art. "The most important thing is not just to be heard, but to inspire in a way that others can find those feelings in themselves and continue them," he says. "It's passing it along because you're inspiring others by what inspired you. I think that's the ideal."

Carlaftes lived on Charles Street in the late 70s and early 80s, moved to San Francisco, and then moved back here to Bleecker Street in 2003. What was the difference between those periods? "It was a lot less chichi back then," he says. "Just a little more solid than other neighborhoods. It was a true village. You can say that now, too, if you didn't know it then. But there's really no more regulars or neighborhood people. And there's nothing new that's lasting. I don't want to complain or seem backwards but I see something that I don't particularly care for." Then he thinks for a moment. "You know, the people that were here before us saw their neighborhood change as well and I'm sure they felt the loss too," he continues. "It's not easy and it takes a lot of work but whatever you're feeling, you've got to rewire yourself and look at it in a positive way."

And these days, even some of Carlaftes' offspring have ended up in the neighborhood. "One of my sons works at Kettle of Fish—which used to be The Lion's Head—on Christopher Street. Drop in and say hello to Dylan. I named him after Dylan Thomas, and his middle name is O'Neill. Now he's around liquor so I don't know how good that is!" he says, laughing.

West Village Original • Theatre

Rainie Cole
January 2014

Photo: Lester Echem

Rainie Cole has been a West Village resident since 1974. With a background in theater, cabaret and television production, Rainie has written, produced, and performed in numerous cabaret shows, including her most successful production "Always, Patsy Cline." She lives on Charles Street with her wife Cindi Creager. Together they run CreagerCole Communications.

Growing up in Cranston, Rhode Island, Rainie Cole harbored a dark secret but hid it well. "I liked girls," she says. "People recall me as always smiling and happy but inside, I was miserable."

Salvation came when she attended the University of New Hampshire and discovered the theatre department. "This decision affected my life in more ways than one," she says. "I became a full-fledged theater and communications major which surprised everyone, as I was always very shy. It was also here that I formed very strong bonds with some guys in the drama department. When we later discovered that we were all gay, my activism began in its own little way. One aspect of it was that I never hid being gay from anyone again."

In 1980, now living in New York, a friend brought Cole to The Duplex, which was then on Grove Street. She fell in love with it. "It was a great combination of gay men and women, and really accepting straight people, all of whom loved music," she says. "I hung out until I was eventually hired. I also worked at Don't Tell Mama uptown. These were perfect jobs as I was paid to entertain. It gave me an opportunity to develop a following and meet people who would then come to see my solo cabaret shows." When The Duplex moved to its current location, the old space became Rose's Turn and Cole chose to remain working there. "I stayed at that cozy, music-filled hole in the wall until it closed in 2007. So for many years, I had the pleasure of walking to work in the best neighborhood in the City."

Cole also discovered another benefit to working in cabarets. "The establishments encouraged you to leave to do shows on the road," she says. "During that time I performed Annie in *Annie Get Your Gun*, Rizzo in *Grease*, and Matron Mama Morton in *Chicago*, all out of town. I was also cast in an Off-Broadway show, *Ten Percent Revue*, which had a successful run at the Actors' Playhouse."

What did she like about performing? "I loved the connection with the audience," she replies. "And I sold a song well. For a long time, between my high energy level and acting, I worked successfully and I made a lot of people happy. That made me happy." However, Cole walked away from performing in 2007, tired of the struggle. "I missed performing for a while," she says. "But I have to admit I didn't go into performing for some of the right reasons. I went into it looking for love." She laughs. "You know, getting all the applause. But I've found joy in expressing myself artistically and being creative in other ways. Now—through the business with Cindi—I'm having fun trying to make things happen for other people."

Cole remembers the day she moved to New York City. "It was September 10, 1974, and we moved into a one-bedroom, rent-stabilized apartment on Charles Street," she recalls. "When my then-girlfriend and I unlocked the door, we took a look at the inviting brick wall, and I said 'It's cute, but we won't stay long.' 39 years later, I'm still here!"

"I loved the Village then because it was where the gay people and artists were," Cole continues. "It's where people like me moved to. But as we know, rents have escalated to the point that artists and young gay people just starting out can't afford our beautiful neighborhood. Something else I regret about the Village: What happened to all the unique shops, cute little bistros, neighborhood bars, and inexpensive holes-in-the-wall? And why did we lose St. Vincent's Hospital?"

"Those are the negatives," she says. "Now let's focus on the positive. I love that the piers we used to call 'Splinter Beach' and 'Tar Beach' have been renovated into beautiful waterside parks. I love the scale of the Village and all the trees. I love the fact that I can see a lot of sky when I walk around my neighborhood. And I love walking the narrow blocks with all the beautiful brownstones. For all that's changed, I still can't imagine calling any other place home."

West Village Original • Theatre

Barbara Garson

April 2013

Photo: Maggie Berkvist

Playwright and author Barbara Garson was born in Brooklyn in 1941. Her plays include "MacBird," her notorious 1966 political parody of "Macbeth," and "Dinosaur Door," an Obie winner in 1977. Her latest book, "Down the Up Escalator: How the 99% Live in the Great Recession," will be published by Doubleday. She lives in Westbeth with her husband, Frank Leonardo.

As a child growing up in Brooklyn, Barbara Garson's parents—one an accountant, the other a bookkeeper—had one thing on their minds. "They were middle-class people who were completely devoted to raising their children," she says. "They weren't artistic and they weren't political, either. They were focused instead on our security."

To illustrate this, Garson tells an amusing story. "One time my mother came to see a play that I wrote," Garson reminisces. "Afterwards she said, 'Gee, those seats were uncomfortable!' My daughter, who was seven at the time, said, 'Grandma, how come you tell everyone how nice Aunt Ina's house is, but Mommy writes a play and all you can say is, 'The seats are uncomfortable?' My mother replied, 'I don't like to encourage her in anything that doesn't earn money.'" Garson laughs. "That was their attitude toward writing and left-wing politics. They weren't necessarily against them. They just wanted me to be financially secure!"

It was while she was an undergraduate at Berkeley in the 60s that both Garson's political awakening and writing career were born. "I had joined the Free Speech movement at Berkeley and we were at a big rally. I made a slip of the tongue and referred to Lady Bird Johnson as Lady MacBird instead of Lady Macbeth. Then the whole thing just clicked and when I had the time, I wrote *Macbird* as a parody of *Macbeth*. It was about the transfer of power after the Kennedy assassination and in the play it appears that Johnson killed him. That, I thought, was a laughable idea and I was quite amazed that people took it seriously. To me, it was a play about two dynasties where one seemed so beautiful (Kennedy) and the other gross (Johnson). All I was saying was listen to them carefully because they're both really saying the same things."

How did *MacBird* make the leap to New York and Off-Broadway? "I came here with the manuscript and showed it to the only person I knew in theatre, a high school classmate," Garson recalls. "His girlfriend decided to produce it but she had no experience either so she brought in a professional. They opened *MacBird* at The Village Gate and filled the cast with people no one had ever heard of: Stacy Keach, Cleavon Little, Bill Devane, and Rue McClanahan. It turned out to be a big success and they all became famous except for me!"

In fact, at the height of her play's success, Garson went as far away as she could. "I worked in an anti-war coffee house at Fort Lewis in Tacoma, Washington," she says. "Back then, my peers and I were against the cult of the personality and celebrity. We didn't want personal publicity." And how does she feel about that now? "Boy, was I wrong!" she says, laughing.

What brought Garson to the Village? "At one point I came back to visit my parents who were still in Brooklyn and saw how much nicer it was to live with them nearby," she says. "So I managed to find an apartment in the Village and, eventually, I moved into Westbeth in 1974. Some people succeed and move to the Village but for me it was the opposite. I think I keep doing the not vastly economically successful things I've always done because Westbeth enables me to do that. As a single parent, I was able to continue to live in the Village and continue to write. Westbeth worked the way it was supposed to for this artist."

As to the changes in the West Village over the years, Garson observes simply, "No one like me could afford to live here now." But when asked if she still enjoys living here, the answer is affirmative. "Oh my God, yes!" she responds. "No matter what happens, the West Village always survives. That's because it's a real neighborhood; so cosmopolitan and intelligent, and yet a neighborhood! When my daughter went away to college, she was really surprised to discover that her classmates not only knew of the West Village, but thought it was so special. That's because it is."

West Village Original • Theatre

David Greenspan
July 2017

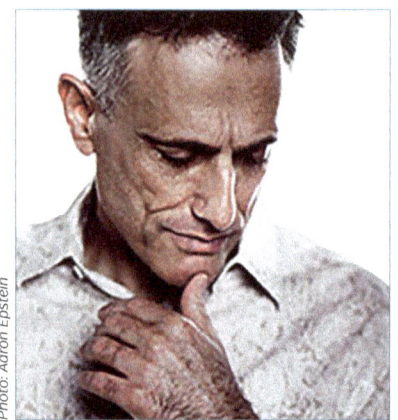

Playwright and actor David Greenspan–born in Los Angeles in 1956–is author of such plays as "She Stoops To Comedy," "Go Back To Where You Are," "The Patsy," and "I'm Looking For Helen Twelvetrees." Greenspan is also the recipient of numerous fellowships. He has won five Obie Awards, including one in 2010 for Sustained Achievement and lives in Westbeth with his longtime partner, painter William Kennon.

Photo: Aaron Epstein

When actor and playwright David Greenspan was a boy growing up in Los Angeles, he would tune into a local radio show called Broadway Showtime. "They used to broadcast Broadway musicals and my father—an aerospace engineer—would record them on his reel-to-reel," he recalls. "I fell in love with them and began checking out other musicals from the library. That was my initial interest in theater. Then I started acting in plays in high school and that's when I determined I was going to go away to both study and act in theater."

"Away" was New York and—after earning a degree in drama at UC Irvine—Greenspan came here in 1978. "I acted in a few plays Off-Off Broadway in theaters that no longer exist," he says. "At a certain point I started making notes in my journal. Those turned into monologues, which I began to perform. This was when I really began to develop as a writer and performer in my own plays. At that time I was also doing a little directing. I did a play by Kathleen Tolan that Joe Papp subsequently brought to the Public Theater. The result was that he put me in residence as a director there in 1989. He was alive during the first year of my residency."

"He was a remarkable guy," Greenspan continues. "He gave me a big opportunity to work before a larger audience. He was very generous to me and I have such fond memories of him. I didn't know him nearly as long as many other people but the time I did was memorable."

Does Greenspan have a preference for either acting or writing? "Not really," he admits. "Acting and writing are both creative activities. I also like all aspects of the theater: writing plays, performing in my plays, and acting in other people's plays as well. I love working with other playwrights. I consider them colleagues and it's a lot of fun to be a part of their vision."

Speaking of life as an actor in New York, Greenspan says, "It's had its ups and downs, both financially and opportunity-wise. I've had a good run of it over the last 15 years though. It's very rewarding, not only the work, but also being part of a larger community. That's a wonderful thing. I have relationships with many actors and directors whom I consider friends. Admittedly, there were a couple of self-indulgent moments when I thought of giving it up, but that was in the past. And that only makes sense if you really, really feel you want to do something else!"

After living together in Jersey City for 15 years, Greenspan and his partner moved into Westbeth in 1999. "We were on a list for ten years before we got in," he says. "We wanted to live in Manhattan and this was the only affordable way to do it. When it finally happened I couldn't believe we were actually living in the West Village. We love it here! We love the building and the sense of community. We got here just before they started renovating the riverfront and once that was complete it made it even better. It's heaven being here."

So the move to New York was a good one? "Yes, it was," Greenspan admits. "When I was young all the TV shows were set in New York and, of course, this was the place for theater. So while there was a point in my life when I had a choice to stay in Los Angeles, it really wasn't a contest. I had always dreamed of coming here and, fortunately, my career has kept me here. Oddly enough, though, my father has never seen me perform in New York. He's still alive, though. He's 99. So maybe he will see me yet!"

West Village Original • Theatre

Robert Heide
January 2018

Photo: George Bonanno

Playwright and author Robert Heide was born and raised in Irvington, New Jersey. The author of numerous plays, Heide has also co-authored many books about collecting memorabilia with his lifetime partner, John Gilman, including three titles for Disney. A West Village resident since 1958, Heide just had a collection of his plays, entitled "Robert Heide: 25 Plays," published by Michael Smith Fast Press.

Growing up with what he describes as a "controlling" father, Robert Heide was able to find his own creative path through, paradoxically, his father's help. "He was the kind of man who said that movies and reading were a waste of time," Heide says. "But I actually think he was a thwarted creative type that felt he had to earn a buck instead. I had piano and art lessons growing up. My father paid my college tuition and when I moved into New York he paid my rent for about a year, and even paid for my acting lessons. So even though he had all sorts of personal issues, he wanted something different for me than what he had."

Heide attended Northwestern University where he studied acting. "I wanted to be Marlon Brando or Jimmy Dean," he says, laughing. "When I came to New York, I studied with Uta Hagen and Stella Adler. However, one day Judith Malina, co-founder of The Living Theatre, said to me, 'You're not an actor. Go home and write a play!' So, I wrote *Hector*, had it staged at the Cherry Lane, and Jerry Tallmer gave me a rave review." This began a string of plays with such titles as *West of the Moon*, *The Bed*, which was also filmed by Andy Warhol, *Crisis of Identity*, and *Suburban Tremens*, appearing either Off-Broadway or at venues like Café Cino, LaMama, and Theatre for the New City.

According to Heide, many of his plays have existential and absurdist turns of people being indifferent to others. Where did that come from?

"I'm not exactly sure," he says. "It's a combination of my life and other people that I know. Edward Albee, who was a friend, once said to me, 'Characters are living in your head that want to be born in a play. They're really pushing you to write.' As for my style, well, I guess I was influenced by Beckett and Pinter. Pinter is always about what's going on underneath the surface. We were all playing it very cool back then. Nobody expressed a lot of emotions in those days. We saw these Bergman and Antonioni films confronting the emptiness of existence and our work reflected that. It was a different kind of theatre."

"It was terrific being in New York and the Village back then," he continues. "Anywhere you went things were happening: at Judson Church, the Night Owl, or Caffe Cino, where I met Bob Dylan. At the Gaslight Café I heard Jack Kerouac, Alan Ginsberg, and Diane di Prima reading their work. You could feel an energy all over the Village. Unlike the 50s where it was about being a rebel without a cause, it was the 60s and we became rebels *with* a cause. That's because we wanted a revolution with love." It was when the shooting at Kent State happened that everything changed. "All hell broke loose in the 70s," Heide says. "It became about the excesses of the bars, discos, and places like Studio 54."

Asked about what he misses from his early days, Heide laughs and responds, "On that I could say practically everything!" However, the passage of time has also afforded him some perspective on life. "Some people like you, some don't," he muses. "It's your human life that's important; who you are and who your friends are. And I understand that human beings are not perfect. We all have a darker side and feel doubt. I recently reread Kierkegaard who suggests taking a leap into blind faith and to focus on positive life. I think that's good advice!"

Referring to his recently published collection of plays, Heide worries that he's campaigning for himself. "But the collection really is a kind of document of the Village in those days," he says. "I'm not bragging about my plays, it's just what we were doing. Like Bob Dylan was just writing his songs. When Dylan received the Nobel Prize, my partner, John, said the prize wasn't for him so much as for Greenwich Village itself. And he's right. That's the turf and that's what it was about!"

West Village Original • Theatre

Gordon Hughes
January 2019

Photo: Vicki Sander

Gordon Hughes, born in Los Angeles in 1941, is a founder of DFB Productions, which manages investments in Broadway, West End, and international theatrical productions. Recent and current Broadway shows include "Peter and the Star Catcher," "An American in Paris," "Come From Away," and "The Cher Show." Hughes and his wife, Barbara, live on Bleecker Street between Perry and Eleventh.

For producer Gordon Hughes, every career he's had was "a logical progression" to his current one. "I went to Cal State University where I studied history, poli sci, and then broadcasting," he says. "When I graduated, the local TV station made me associate producer on a show called *Ralph Story's Los Angeles*. But my goal was to get into TV so I jumped over to sales. That's where I learned to write and produce commercials. When I did end up as director of broadcasting in a TV station, I learned contracts as well as working with the unions. And agents! Some were a treat."

Making a switch to the print, which brought him to New York in 1990, Hughes was with ABP Magazines for sixteen years until he realized he missed the entertainment industry. "I was kind of tired and bored with what I was doing," he says. "I had a very good friend who was the only guy I could talk to about theater, television, actors, etc. One year we went to the Edinburgh Fringe Festival and saw about four plays a day for a week. I thought it was fabulous! So he and I and two other guys formed Direct From Broadway."

Their first play was *La Bête*. "I was like a babe in the woods," Hughes says. "This was a story of Moliere done in couplets. Can you imagine such a thing?" He stayed the course, though, and succeeded. "It's been a great ride and right now I'm happy to be involved with *Come From Away*, which is still running," he says. "I didn't think it was going to be anything like what's happening to it now. They've handled the marketing on that so well, but it was word of mouth that drove that show. I also just opened *The Cher Show* and I'm an investor in that, not a producer. I did it for two reasons: I really think Cher's story is better than any of the other so-called jukebox musicals and to work with [producer] Jeffrey Seller is amazing."

So it transpires that all of Hughes' skills acquired over a lifetime have come in handy in the theatre. Does he have any words of wisdom? "I always say there are three kinds of investors: those that want to discover talent, those that want to have their photograph taken with Cher and get their names in the program, and the idiots who actually think they're going to make money," he says, laughing. "I'm in the first group: I love to discover talent. Just to be able to look at actors and directors and say, 'I helped that career!' is wonderful. And another thing, I didn't go into this business to thump my chest. I don't even put my name in the *Playbill* anymore. I mean, I like my friends to know what I'm doing but I try to go stealth."

"This is not necessarily a young man's game," he continues. "I've been very fortunate in life and once you can put the money together you get to do something like this, which I love. It's not a retirement job by any stretch of the imagination, but it's just not as hard as working at a television network. You feel more liberated and you don't need to suit up. We're like gypsies."

Even though he "always knew about Greenwich Village," Hughes didn't move here until 20 years ago. "I'm vexed by what's happened here since then," he says. "There were a lot of VW buses with peace signs on them and now it's all Range Rovers. That's why I go to Mucho Gusto café on Hudson Street. It's full of old hippies. We all know each other, chat together, and it's really fun."

And yet, it's the mix of old places and new that make the neighborhood so appealing to Hughes. "I love hanging out in old places like the Vanguard, Smalls, and the Bus Stop, and then doing a change up and having a nice dinner at the Waverly Inn," he says. "I recently had to go to dinner at a very chichi restaurant on the Upper East Side and I thought, 'I couldn't live here any more than I could live on Mars. The men still wear their hair like Cary Grant did!'"

West Village Original • Theatre

Penny Jones
February 2012

Born in Minneapolis in 1929, Penny Jones is founder and creator of Penny Jones & Company Puppets. Since the 1970's, the company has specialized in informal puppet shows for children as well as puppet ballets with live music for audiences of all ages. A West Village resident for decades who now lives in Westbeth, Jones still performs regularly.

When Penny Jones attended Antioch College in the 1950s, part of the requirement for students was participating in "co-op" jobs in which they experienced different careers. "I was sick of everything by my senior year and I really wanted something new and exotic," she says. "So I applied to work as a puppeteer in a department store in Providence, Rhode Island. They agreed, but first sent me to New York for a two-day crash course in handling puppets at Suzari Marionettes. Then we went off to Providence and I did twenty shows a day, eight minutes a show." It turned out to be a work experience that would determine her life's passion.

Jump to 1970, when Jones was by then working with a quality puppet company. She was also a mother with a young son and was taking him to various puppet shows. "They were terrible," she says. "They were staffed with actors who behaved as if children's theatre was beneath them. The scripts were poor, the characters stupid. I became very committed to the idea that when I had my own troop I was going to specialize in shows for younger children. I spent the rest of my life exploring different ways to reach younger children, to inspire and include them. The wonderful thing about children is they naturally participate. You almost have to hold them back and if you invite them to be part of a show they just love it."

It wasn't long before The Little Synagogue on East 20th Street invited her to do a puppet show. "I asked my puppetry class at The New School if they wanted to become a troupe and they agreed," she says. "We paid a percentage of the box office to cover the rent." Jones proceeded to mount consecutive repertory seasons at the The Little Synagogue, The Studio on West 11th Street and Greenwich House Music School, and monthly appearances at the Barnes & Noble children's department at Fifth Avenue and 18th Street. During this period she created nine puppet shows all designed specifically for younger children. "The production cost was mostly for labor since the materials were cheap and the theatrical effects simple," she says. "And while we dealt with serious themes for some shows, it was all couched in language a three year old could relate to."

Why does Jones feel that puppetry suits her so well? "I'm a natural storyteller," she says. "It comes without difficulty. I could have been a writer, I'm sure. I'm a very curious and adventurous person, as well. I like to experiment with all kinds of different materials for my puppets. I also love making stuff. Doing a puppet show includes all the things that I love to do so it fits me to a 't'. However, I never used to call myself an artist and for years I had this room in my apartment but I never called it my studio. Then one day I finally said, 'You know what? I *am* an artist and this *is* my studio!'"

Nothing better illustrates the change to the West Village than Jones' audience members themselves. "When I first came to Westbeth and did a puppet show here there weren't any children," she says. "Now there's this tidal wave of young kids. It's a good time to do repertory puppet shows. All these children are a plus to me now in my career." And while Jones could list "all the negative things" that she regrets have happened to this neighborhood over the years, it's her memories of an earlier time that resonate.

"When I first moved here what I loved about the Village was how pretty and charming the streets and buildings were," she reminisces. "You would pass these wonderful little curiosity shops where people were doing their own thing. I was extremely happy, too, because I could wear whatever I wanted to wear and just blend in. I wore these kind of Greek sandals that were made by a local shoe-maker and nobody looked twice. Everybody else was wearing them, too. The Village was like a family. It was my kind of place, all blissful and peaceful. It was a very lovely time, as if summer would never end."

West Village Original • Theatre

Erwin Lerner

September 2015

Playwright and screenwriter Erwin Lerner–born in the Bronx in 1935–is the author of such plays as "Dilemma," "Katz' Poem," and "Happy New Year, Love." Lerner served in the Air Force before moving back to New York and, eventually, Greenwich Village. Lerner met his wife of 43 years, Mary T. Phillips, when they lived across the courtyard from each other on West 10th Street. Today they reside on Morton Street.

For Erwin Lerner, his desire to become a playwright was put on hold for a number of years while he explored other options. "If I had worked in the post office my uncultured middle-class family would have been very happy," he says. "I quit high school when I was 16 and joined the Air Force. When I got out, my mother—who was working for L'Oreal of Paris at the time—convinced me to become a hairdresser. She thought it would straighten me out! I went along with it and became excellent at it. But I was more interested in developing my mind and I just wanted to be a playwright."

When that finally came about, Lerner's plays were produced off-off Broadway. But according to him it was a difficult journey. "People Off-Off-Broadway were all very left wing and I was proud of my military status so that made me an outlaw in theatre culture in the Village," he says. "They were all dealing with the anti-war movement and Vietnam and I had no problem with either. It made me a pariah, but I just kept doing my thing. I would find a director and we'd get a cast together and do a number performances. Throughout it all, I was growing up."

Lerner claims that the "stifled intelligence level" of society and civilization are what he was trying to depict in his plays. "But I wanted to enlighten people without being boring or giving them a lecture," he says. "My plays are funny and about the idea that there's no solution to life's problems. I had this play where the characters would just run around in circles." As for his writing process, as he got into a play he found he would start to live it. "I was in the world of the play. I would go where it took me. When it was over I would rewrite and edit until I finally finished it. My plays are very sharp. I feel like I took theater in a different direction. And while my style impressed a lot of people it pissed a lot of people off, too," he says, laughing.

What drew Lerner to Greenwich Village? "I was aware of the word 'Bohemia' but I thought I never could be a part of it because I was too uneducated at the time," he says. "Then I got to the Village and started reading and expanding my brain. I became intellectual, philosophical, historical, and everything that I thought I should become. I became educated and I started to understand the universe a little bit. The world all around me was just so interesting. Up until my first play, I was a very insecure person. But the reaction to it was so good I remember thinking when I got back to my apartment that I would never be afraid of anything again in my life. And I've been feeling that way since."

When asked how much the West Village has changed since he moved here 52 years ago, Lerner laughingly exclaims, "The rich got richer and the poor got outta here!" Then he becomes serious. "There's been an immensity of money that's changed everything," he observes. "Things have gotten prettier, of course, but at the same time there are a lot of boarded up shops, so that's an odd juxtaposition. A lot of money came over from Europe and the buildings they bought into were expensive. This new generation has a lot of money. A lot of it is inherited and of course that kind of money earns a lot by itself."

These days, Lerner is tethered to an oxygen tank all the time as he suffers from emphysema. Yet he remains upbeat and happy to be in the West Village. "I'm a hermit here but I make the most of it," he declares. "I'm on my computer. I'm writing a phantasmagoric memoir, not really my life but rather my life with a different dimension. I'm relating with my wife. We've had this wonderful marriage for 43 years and I'm very lucky. Given what I started with I like to think that I helped create my life as it is. That gives me a good sense of my creativity. And I keep going."

West Village Original • Theatre

Marshall W. Mason

March 2019

Marshall W. Mason–born in Amarillo, Texas in 1940–co-founded the Circle Rep in New York and was its artistic director for 18 years. On and Off Broadway he directed such hits as "The Hot L Baltimore," "Fifth of July," "Talley's Folly," "As Is," and "Burn This." Nominated five times for a Tony Award for directing, in 2016 he received a special Tony for Lifetime Achievement.

"I was headed for the theatre at birth," says director Marshall W. Mason. "I was sure I was going to be an actor. I did my first play when I was seven and I loved it." However, it was a youthful experience that made Mason aware of another possibility. "When I was about nine years old I saw the movie *Pinky*. It was a really powerful film about a black woman passing for white and I was profoundly moved by it. The credits listed the director as Elia Kazan. I didn't know what a director was, but I went to school the next day and announced, 'My favorite director is Elia Kazan!'"

An important first step on Mason's journey was deciding to go to Northwestern University. "I studied acting for a couple of years, but it turned out I wasn't very good at it," he says. "So, I thought, 'Uh-oh. It's law for me!' But another teacher asked me if I had considered other roles, like writing. 'No talent in that,' I replied. What about directing? Well, there *was* a play I wanted to direct, Williams' *Cat on a Hot Tin Roof*. It dealt with issues that resonated with me: my sexual identity, football because I'm from Texas, and Maggie and her poverty because my family was very poor and I got a full scholarship to Northwestern. My production of *Cat* was a tremendous success and so I thought, 'Apparently I'm a director!'"

Mason moved to Manhattan in 1961, where he began working in the burgeoning Off-Off-Broadway theater movement in venues such as

Caffe Cino and LaMama. "I found my voice at Caffe Cino," he says. "I did my first play in New York there." It was also where Mason would meet playwright Lanford Wilson, thus inaugurating a lengthy and very successful writer/director partnership. "Lanford was quite flattered that I'd seen all his plays," he says. "Ultimately, I think we were so successful because we started off with honesty, which was really important in our subsequent years together. He and I had the longest professional collaboration in the history of American theatre. That was certified by *Playbill* about halfway through our career."

Why does Mason think he has such an affinity for directing? "I think because watching actors performing and creating right in front of your eyes always excited me," he says. "When I realized I wasn't such a great actor myself, I also realized that I could help actors achieve more than they thought they could. I was really an actor's director for the first years. It wasn't until I met Lanford that I began to shift toward being a playwright's director as well in terms of helping them with their structure, characterization, and dialogue. It's bridging those two worlds between playwright and actor that the director facilitates, turning the play into a living thing."

In 1969 Mason and Wilson would join Tanya Berezin and Rob Thirkield to found Circle Rep, originally housed on the Upper West Side. "We were called The American Theatre Project at first but it was suggested we call ourselves Circle Theatre. We agreed, but I was afraid that we would be confused with Circle in the Square. We, in fact, were confused with them throughout our whole existence," he says, laughing. In 1974 they moved downtown to the old Sheridan Square Theatre and spent the next twenty years there. "We immediately became a Village institution," Mason says. "Bringing a theatre back to life is a big deal. In addition, we had a wonderful audience and strong subscription list."

Mason lays much of that success to the special qualities of the neighborhood itself. "The West Village back then was quite wonderful," he admits. "It was a very supportive, encouraging, and convivial atmosphere. We felt a little bit like the Impressionists with the kind of camaraderie that existed among those artists who invented a whole new way of looking at painting. I still consider a café on Christopher Street my office, even though I've moved to Jersey City. And being a Tony voter brings me into the City to see everything on Broadway. People always say, 'Oh, how wonderful that you get to do that!'" He laughs. "Sometimes!"

West Village Original • Theatre

Scott Morfee

November 2016

Photo: Karly Fischer

Scott Morfee is the founding producer of Barrow Street Theater in Greenwich House. Born in Boston in 1954 and raised in Pittsburgh, as a producer Morfee has presented such hits as "Buyer & Cellar," "The Flick," "Red Light Winter," "Bugs," and "Killer Joe." In addition, he and BST have presented over 100 shows and guest artists from around the world. Scott currently lives on Barrow Street as well.

Scott Morfee's passion for theater was not, as one might expect, something that consumed him since childhood. Rather, it gradually evolved after he moved to New York in 1977. "I grew to love theater and the performing arts, but it took a long time," he says. "I wasn't born with this interest and not only didn't I study it in school, I barely cared about it when I first moved to New York! It happened as I lived here."

Morfee went straight into marketing and public relations after arriving. "All told, I spent at least 10 or 12 years in that field and I learned a lot about the business," he says. "Sort of on a parallel track I was seeing more and more arts and theater and it was becoming very important to me. Eventually, the company I was working for was sold. I thought it was a good time to leave and try to promote and market plays. And by that time I knew theatre was something I loved."

How did he finally make the leap? "In the late 80s, some friends and I decided to produce a play in Los Angeles, of all places," Morfee recalls. "I was not a terribly effective producer back then but we got the show up. I returned to New York and worked on a couple of projects as an associate producer. Then in 1998 a friend called and asked me if I wanted to raise half the money to produce a play called *Killer Joe* by Tracy Letts at the Soho Playhouse. I said 'yes.'"

Killer Joe turned out to be a big hit. "It was one of those great experiences," Morfee says. "It was a fabulous time for Off-Broadway. People would come to New York to see *Hedwig and the Angry Inch* and *Killer Joe*, bypassing Broadway altogether. There was so much really cool stuff going on down here. If you combine the jazz, theatre, and piano bar culture it was like the Miracle Mile." In 2003, Morfee found out that the theatre space in Greenwich House was available. "I literally ran there and we took the lease over in October of that year," he says.

So Morfee went from being a "not terribly effective" producer to one who was demonstrably effective, starting his own theatre company, and producing other hits like *Bugs* and *Buyer & Cellar*. Can he say that *Killer Joe* is what finally turned his interest into a passion? "The show taught me a lot," he admits. "I personally filled many positions during the run: lead producer, box office manager, house manager, usher, and more. So it was pretty immersive and its success made my decision to try it again much easier. I found myself sticking with it because it's so challenging. And as they say, 'You're only as good as your last show.' That's motivating!"

Since Morfee began the Barrow Street Theatre, the real estate boom in the Village has put its own kind of pressure on the industry. "We've lost quite a few venues," Morfee says. "Converted to condominiums or just gone. That's the sad part. The good part is knowing how many people from around the world come to see what we're doing at our theatre. There are times when fifty percent of our audiences are from outside both the metro area and the country. A lot of that has to do with our international programming. But we also have a profile for good work and the brand has earned the respect of people who live outside the city. That to me is fantastic."

In other words, it's the idea of the Village as a destination? "Absolutely," he agrees. "I think part of the intimacy of our theater and the homespun vibration of it is what makes people come back over and over again. You get to enjoy a neighborhood as well. It's experiential, but in a uniquely West Village way."

West Village Original • Theatre

Dina Paisner
March 2016

Dina Paisner has been a resident of Bank Street since the 1940s and worked for decades as a model and professional actor. As a model, she has appeared in various magazines and periodicals including New York Magazine and The New York Times. Her acting credits include film, television, "Medea" on Broadway with Irene Papas, and many Off-Broadway and regional productions

When actor and model Dina Paisner was born in Brooklyn's Bedford Stuyvesant neighborhood it was, according to her, very sleepy and peaceful. "I went to P.S. 25," she says. "It was a very old school on Lafayette Avenue. The toilets were outside and we had to leave the building to use them." When, exactly, was this? "No, thank you! I'm reluctant to give my age. People immediately put you into a category as a result and I don't like to be categorized. Let's just say I'm way up there," she says, laughing.

Paisner grew up as the youngest of seven children of a family that had emigrated from the Ukraine. "My father was a Hebrew teacher," she recalls. "My family was a real kind of tragic family out of a Chekov play. When I was a child I would observe them all sitting around on Friday nights with the candles lit. There was so much quiet tension that I felt compelled to break it. So I would imitate all my neighbors and make everybody laugh. Everyone thought I was going to be an artist but I loved theatre more and that's what I pursued." As an actor, Paisner was very busy for a while, going from one role to another. She was particularly active Off-Broadway before it became "fashionable."

What is it about the theatre that appeals so much to her? "Because it's life," she says emphatically. "Theatre is life! Theatre saved my life, actually. Like so many children I had unfortunate things happen to me that kind of scarred me a little bit. I compensated with theater and

I was able to live my life through it. And I was a very good actress." Were these childhood traumas the reason she never had children of her own? "I was always waiting to grow up before I had kids of my own," she says. "I never wanted to inflict my problems on another generation. That said, I love my family and I've always loved people. I've never been afraid of them."

In 2006, Paisner discovered that eighteen of her lymph nodes had become cancerous. After treatment, she had seven years remission but recently her health has dwindled precariously and she is now in hospice care in her home. "I'm not depressed, though, because I have so much to do and I don't have that luxury," she says, paradoxically. "I find that my relationships with people are on a much deeper level because the distractions of pursuing a career are gone. My decisions are much easier now. My life is quickly shedding unnecessary things and in some ways it's on a higher quality because my days are so precious. It's like the worse my health gets the better my spirits get. I don't advise getting sick in order to make the quality of your life better but there's no turning back now!"

Paisner has lived on Bank Street since the 1940s in a "tiny, old studio" she inherited from a sister-in-law. "I've seen a lot of changes," she admits. "When I walk through the neighborhood it's almost like I see in 3D. I see the building that was there before and the one before that. I miss a lot of the old Village institutions like the Mom and Pop stores and the barbershops. But I'm thrilled to still be here. There are a few old-timers still around and we help each other out. I have a neighbor who feeds my cat three times a day. And while it's become so expensive here, I was brought up in the Depression so I can live very frugally."

Does Paisner have any words of advice for others? "Whatever happens in life, there's always a funny side to it so having a sense of humor is very important," she says. "And being creative is paramount. The greatest gift in life is to be creative. That's because your mind gets out of the way. You act very naturally on your impulses, which come from a very universal force within. So stay creative, everybody," she urges, laughing. "Hang loose and get out of your own head!"

West Village Original • Theatre

Everett Quinton

March 2010

Actor and director Everett Quinton has lived on Morton Street since 1975. That same year he met Charles Ludlam, founder of the Ridiculous Theatrical Company on Sheridan Square, and they became life partners and collaborators until Mr. Ludlam's death in 1987. Today, Quinton still acts regularly as well as directs.

Photo: Everett Quinton

Born in Brooklyn in 1951, actor Everett Quinton grew up in Park Slope, as he puts it, "On the poor side of Seventh Avenue." According to him, Brooklyn was pretty provincial then, despite its proximity to Manhattan. "When you went to take the subway," he recalls, "the signs read 'To Coney Island' or 'The City'. Not 'Manhattan'. I was even surprised that people actually lived in Manhattan. I thought it was all just businesses and towering office buildings. To then discover these interesting neighborhoods nestled inside all of that was quite amazing. I was fascinated by it."

Discovering the West Village in particular gave Quinton a sense of freedom, especially with regards to his sexuality. "When I found the West Village," he says, "I vowed to myself, 'No more closet queen! I don't know what's going to happen here but there's going to be no more girl friends and no more lying for me.'" He and Ludlam met on Christopher Street, right next to the Lucille Lortel Theatre, then known as the Theatre de Lys. "Charles's name is on the Theatre Walk of Fame right outside the theater," Quinton says. "Although someone once asked me why his name is so far from everyone else's. It's because I met him on that very spot. He introduced himself and within a year we moved in together on Morton Street."

Quinton's debut with the Ridiculous Theatrical Company was on February 10, 1976 in a show called *Caprice*. "For some reason, I always remember the date. Maybe because I played a ballerina who gets abducted!" he says, laughing. "It was a last-minute role for me. I was in the theater one day but off in a corner, finishing a term paper for a class at Hunter College. Charles approached me and said that he had written a role but there was no one to fill it. He asked me if I would do it. Since I had been watching rehearsals regularly and was familiar with the play, I agreed. That started my performing career."

After that, Quinton began getting regular roles in Ludlam's company. "A bigger role in *Caprice* came open, which I auditioned for but didn't get," he says. "Then at one point Charles did *Der Ring Gott Farbinjet*. I didn't have to audition for that because there were so many roles. Instead, I lobbied for a particular one and got it. Then I showed that I could deliver the goods, so I never had to audition again. I got a company position." From there he was involved in most of the company's iconic productions, including the aforementioned *Ring* plus *Galas, Camille, The Mystery of Irma Vep*, and *The Artificial Jungle*, winning awards for his performances.

What was the Village like when he moved here? "It was right after Stonewall so there was a sense of neighborhood," he says. Then he corrects himself. "There *still* is a sense of neighborhood. It's just that I found it to be more self-contained in those days. You didn't need to go anywhere because you could get everything in this neighborhood! There was the Capezio shop on MacDougal Street, where you could buy leotards and dance shoes for a show. Or those two beautiful art supply stores, one on West Fourth Street and one on Greenwich Street. There were two fish markets—as well as Zito's Breads—on Bleecker Street. They all got eaten up by time."

Quinton stops and laughs. "I have to be careful that I don't start sounding like an old man," he says, "complaining about how this has changed and that has changed! Besides, I think the West Village will be just fine. And sometimes it just takes time to get used to certain things. Take those glass towers on Charles Street at the river, for example. I am now beginning to accept a certain beauty about them. And what can you do? They are there. Time marches on, and who's the arbiter of beauty? Certainly not me."

West Village Original • Theatre

William Repicci

December 2011

Kenya, 2006; Photo: Virgilio Pante

Bill Repicci, born in Batavia, NY, has taught school in northern Kenya, run programs for the developmentally disabled in Alaska, produced over 25 plays in New York ("Swingtime Canteen," "Jodie's Body," "Squonk"), been CEO of a dramatic publishing company, and recently returned to Africa and then Southeast Asia on a two-year humanitarian project. He was just hired as President and CEO of the Lymphatic Education & Research Network (LE&RN).

Growing up in a small town in western New York, Bill Repicci not only had dreams of seeing the world, but the support of his parents that empowered him to make his own way and follow those dreams. "My mother would always say, 'Never be afraid to do the things you need to do to be happy'," he recalls. "And my father, no matter what I told him I was going to do, would always give me his blessing."

This blessing was just what he needed when—as he was graduating with a degree in philosophy from LeMoyne College in the 70s—a unique opportunity arose. "I ended up teaching English and history at a secondary school in Mandera, Kenya," he says. "It was on the Somali-Ethiopian border and the Kenyans had found it impossible to engage locals to teach there due to the constant tribal warfare. It was a wonderful and challenging adventure for me, though. After two years, I returned to the States and was introduced to an organization that was working with people who were developmentally disabled. This was an exciting era of change in that field and it led me to pursue graduate work in Scandinavia and to become a psychologist. For the next fifteen years this would be the focus of my life, including nine years as executive director of the Fairbanks Resource Agency in Alaska."

So how did Repicci segue from running an organization for the developmentally disabled in Alaska to producing theatre in New York? "While I was living in Alaska," he recalls, "I also had a sublet in New

York. One year I saw a riveting play here called *Creeps*, written by a man with cerebral palsy. It was about the frustration of individuals with that disorder trying to live on equal terms in society. I brought the cast up to Alaska and produced the play throughout the state to inspire a change in attitudes and program models." The success of that turned into a U.S. tour, after which Repicci made a decision. In 1987 he came back to New York for good, bought an apartment on Horatio Street, and immersed himself in theatre. "As it happens, one night I was introduced to John Glines who had produced *Torch Song Trilogy*," he says. "We became great friends and began producing together."

At that time, Sheridan Square was the epicenter of his world. "Here I found a sense of freedom I had never experienced before," he says. Much of his personal and professional exploits over the next several years would occur right around that area. He would go on to produce numerous plays at the Grove Street Theatre and Actors Playhouse. He would record an album with Marie Blake, who played piano for many years at The 5 Oaks on Grove Street. And he would produce a documentary called *The Ladies of Grove Street,* which featured Marie, as well as Gladys Easter and Arthur's Tavern pianist, Mabel Godwin. "For me, the day started at Pennyfeathers for breakfast and it meant a BLT at the Riviera for lunch," he says. "It meant being at one of my shows at night and then going to The 5 Oaks, or the Monster, or the Duplex with friends afterwards, capped off by a 4 a.m. snack at Tiffany's. It was a wonderful, contained world that I rarely had to leave."

When asked how the West Village has changed over the years, Repicci offers a unique insight. "What makes that an elusive question to answer is that one has to factor in how they have changed as well," he says. "It's easy to see the changes, but actually I think I began to change even before the Village did. So many of the places I used to frequent are gone now. The theatres I used to produce in have disappeared. But in reality I had stopped going to those places, and I had stopped producing in the Village in favor of theaters uptown. So as I got older I left a lot of that romantic past behind even before it disappeared on its own. The bittersweet melancholy that I might feel comes not only from looking back fondly on a era that has passed, but one that I've moved on from as well."

West Village Original • Theatre

Salvador Peter Tomas

March 2015

Photo: Maggie Berkvist

Opera singer, narrator, actor, and director Salvador Peter Tomas was born in Pass Christian, Mississippi in 1920. Tomas is an alumnus of The Juilliard School, Trinity College in London, and the Fontainebleau School in France. As an opera singer, his repertoire includes standard bass baritone roles and as a narrator, he narrated Honegger's "Le Roi David" for over twenty years in recital halls and theaters around the country.

When he was seven years old, Salvador Peter Tomas' mother—in response to his father's affair with a local woman and the ensuing scandal—whisked him and his six sisters to New York City. "It was a good reason to leave," Tomas says. "We were part of the exodus leaving a South full of violent racial prejudice. I don't even remember preparing to leave; it was so sudden. The traumatic thing that has colored my whole life is saying goodbye to my father on the train. I said to him, 'I'll never see you again!' That happened to be true and after that I was looking for my father all of my life."

Tomas' mother eventually bought a house in Queens where they settled down and he could pursue his joy of singing. "I was always singing," he says. "I was in the glee club, the drama club, and in operettas throughout junior and high school." After his WWII service in Europe where he was part of the Signal Corps attached to aviation, Tomas took advantage of the G.I. Bill to attend Trinity College in London and study voice and drama. "I was in a graduation performance at Trinity and I was so well received," he says. "They said to me, 'We didn't think you could do it.' That was a nice compliment! People were always telling me they didn't think I could do it. It was because I got roles that were not ordinarily assigned to a person of color."

Aside from having the talent, how did he manage to land those roles? "Because I went into the arts, music, and opera, I always associated with people who are on the better side of living," he explains. "They have access to more money, more education, and to each other's help. So they helped me as well." It was this combination of people taking an interest in him and then using their influence that advanced Tomas' career. "That's how I got a scholarship to Fontainebleau," he says. "And it was the interest of people at Juilliard that gave me the opportunity to narrate almost 100 performances of Le Roi David over the years. I made a career just out of that. Don't get me wrong. There are crappy people everywhere. But that's the wonderful thing about being a human being. You never know when you're going to find another fantastic one!"

Tomas moved into Westbeth when it opened in 1970 and remembers a different world. "It was a run down waterfront, just like Marseille," he says. "A no man's land. The elevated highway was still there and the gay traffic was incredible. There were bars on 14th Street, lots of clubs and a huge multi-level gay disco just a couple of blocks from here. Although the piers were boarded up they would always be broken into and orgies went on in them. Then there were the parked trucks down here where guys would carry on as well. For myself, I never overdid anything and I mostly kept away from that."

It wasn't just the gay scene, though, that characterized the area. "Artists from all over the city came to the Village and to Westbeth in particular," Tomas says. "They made it a very lively, buzzing place. Many people were able to function, blossom, and realize their own potential without the pressure of earning lots of money. And the landlords left you alone when they thought their property was not worth anything."

How different is it now? "Suddenly, these same landlords only want people with a lot of money and those aren't struggling artists. And the landlords won because the story of the West Village—and all New York—is real estate. It's become a rich man's paradise." Yet Tomas still manages to find a vestige of the area he moved into 45 years ago. "It's great. It's the Village and it's New York! I still love it and I've been here a long time." He pauses for a second. "Although age does not go without retribution from Mother Nature. She's causing me a lot of problems!" he says, laughing.

West Village Original • Theatre

David Van Asselt
January 2009

Playwright David Van Asselt was born in Lancaster, Pennsylvania in 1950. David is the author of such works as "Winning," "A Trip to the Beach," "Dog Daze," and "A Fable." He is also the founding Artistic Director of Rattlestick Playwrights Theater on Waverly Place, which is celebrating its 15th anniversary this year.

It took playwright David Van Asselt a couple of tries before he found a career he could flourish in. "I first went to NYU to study film," he says. "Then I went back to NYU and studied Philosophy with the idea to teach. But I soon realized that didn't sound very appealing to me. So, I went and built houses for a while but I got bored with that, too. Since I've always been interested in theatre, I started to write plays while doing carpentry. One play was produced here so I thought I would give New York another try. It didn't take me long to realize I didn't know nearly enough about theater, so I gave myself a crash course: assistant director, carpenter, designer, manager, etc. I did a lot of everything!"

It also didn't take long for Van Asselt to realize how important networking was. So, he started a group of seven playwrights who met regularly and read each other's work. "Inevitably these meetings turned into gripe sessions," he says. "We complained that theatres weren't presenting a lot of new work which, at that time, was true. After a while I got kind of tired listening to this and said, 'Why don't we start a theatre company ourselves?' So, Rattlestick was born. And right from the beginning it was about promoting younger playwrights; ones that I felt needed to be heard. And I absolutely enjoyed that part of it."

Finding their current space turned out to be a case of serendipity. "In 1994, when we did our first play here, the space was known as Theatre Off Park and it was a rental house," Van Asselt recalls. "We had a successful show running in a midtown theater, but we wanted to extend it. It happened that this theater was going to be dark that whole summer, so I grabbed it. I thought it was kind of a nice spot for us. It wasn't Theatre Row. Rather, it was a place where you could actually establish an identity as a theater company." After two years of booking the theater for all their productions, the opportunity arose for them to take over the lease and they jumped at it.

Of course, it helps to have a landlord one can work with and Rattlestick has been blessed (pun intended) with the cooperation of theirs: St. John's in the Village Episcopal Church. "One of the reasons we can stay in this space is that St. John's has been a terrific landlord," Van Asselt admits. "They've worked with us to keep the rent at a reasonable rate. All of the theaters downtown are closing because rents are being so jacked up, so it's nice to have someone who's not just thinking about money. In the theater, you have to have some angels."

Does Van Asselt think that their theater's presence in the West Village influences their choice of plays? "I think so, yes," he says. "In the sense that we've been able to be a lot more adventurous and a lot more challenging. Again, a big part of that is because we have St. John's support. They've never attempted any censorship whatsoever. And also because we tied into the West Village tradition of being Bohemian and experimental." Is that tradition still alive? "Not so much anymore," Van Asselt has to admit. "It has changed tremendously here. If anything, Rattlestick has probably lost a little of our audience because the Village has been scaled up so dramatically as of late. Unlike the old-time Villagers, I don't think the new Villagers are necessarily theatergoers. I think they just want to go to very fancy restaurants!"

Van Asselt punctuates this observation with one of those small, personal stories that best illuminate the kind of seismic shifts the West Village has gone through recently. "The old Waverly Inn restaurant was a wonderful place to hang out in," he says. "It was just down the street, and I could drop in after a show and the cook would whip up a plate of jambalaya for me. We did a lot of cross marketing for each other, too. They lost the lease a few years ago and a very posh restaurant went in. Suddenly, it became a very different atmosphere and we were excluded. Perhaps, as they get more established, the new restaurant will be a little more willing to embrace other aspects of the Village. But for now, it's sort of a sad thing."

One Jackson Square

> *While I love the historic and low-rise character of this neighborhood, I am somewhat tired of derivative red-brick buildings being built to look like something old. I believe you can retain the character of this neighborhood and still have some interesting and forward-looking architecture.*
>
> —Rick Meyerowitz

West Village Original • Visual Arts

Isabel Case Borgatta
June 2015

Sculptor Isabel Case Borgatta was born in Madison, Wisconsin in 1921. In her lengthy career, she has had numerous solo and group exhibitions, seen her pieces in museum, corporate and private collections, and been the recipient of numerous awards, among them Yaddo and Edward McDowell Fellowships. Borgatta moved into Westbeth in 1986 and still maintains her studio there.

When she was 12 years old, Isabel Case Borgatta made a carving in Ivory Soap and won a national prize of $100 in the popular contest sponsored by Procter & Gamble. "One hundred dollars was a big deal in the depths of the Depression and I think I became a sculptor because of that," she says, laughing. "I started carving anything I could get my hands on. I went from soap to stone! But I think I always had a feeling for form and volume and I liked to make shapes."

Borgatta went on to attend both Smith College and Yale, from which she graduated with a degree in sculpture. "It's not the most popular major but it was mine and I loved it," she says. "And I had a blast! I mean, a girl at Yale? Come on! I was doing what I really loved to do and nobody was holding me back." After Yale she came to New York and started doing 'direct' carving. "That was something new," she says. "Before that people had built things up in clay models and copied that. I worked directly from a raw piece of stone without preliminary drawings or models." Since then, Borgatta has shown her work consistently. "I've shown pretty much all over the world," she says. "I'm not a superstar, but I'm up there."

According to Borgatta, the piece of stone itself is where she finds her inspiration. "Sometimes I have something in mind that I want to carve," she says. "More often, I find a stone that's *simpatico* and I want to work with it. I love the tactile and sensual quality of stone. I can walk into a room with 100 stones and pick out the ones I like very quickly. Something about the shape, size, color, and texture will speak to me. But I'm open to a lot of modifications as I work. I like the fact that stone doesn't let you make very many mistakes. You can't put anything back once it's off. It's a tough discipline!"

It's this dedication that sustained Borgatta at a time when women artists were all but ignored by mainstream galleries and museums. "Women artists were not taken seriously when I was starting out," she says. "They didn't show women at all! People don't know that now because there's been such a change, but the opportunities were just about zero. That's one reason that I became active in the women's movement." Does Borgatta feel she missed opportunities as a result of such misogyny? "No, I feel like I was in the group that helped make a change," she says. "This is what the organization Women in the Arts was all about: to promote opportunities for women so they could show their work. As a result, so much progress has been made."

When Borgatta first moved to New York in the 1940s she lived on Christopher Street. Her marriage to another artist led them to raise their three children in Westchester County and, after separating from her husband, she moved back to the city and subsequently to Westbeth. "To me the Village was always very much like home," she says. "I liked the scale, the smaller buildings, and the informality. I liked the fact that you could make friends in the neighborhood as well as in your own building. I liked that there were a number of other artists around. I had never completely lost touch with the neighborhood even though I had spent those years in Dobbs Ferry. In fact, I showed at the Whitney way back when it was on 8th Street and now I'm looking forward to going to the new one right around the corner!"

As an artist and a resident of Westbeth, Borgatta seems to have found the ideal neighborhood to both live and work in. "I think it's more tolerant of everybody and everything, more relaxed, less demanding, and more accepting," she says. "I just feel more at ease here. I love the lifestyle." She pauses for second. "I still think the West Village is the heart of Manhattan for what matters to me."

West Village Original • Visual Arts

Marjorie Colt
September 2014

Painter and long-time West Villager Marjorie Colt was born in Canton, Ohio in 1935. Colt moved to Horatio Street in 1959 and started running a B&B out of her house there in 1992. After selling the building this summer, Colt moved permanently to Oakland, California to be closer to her three children.

When Marjorie Colt was a girl growing up in the Midwest, her dream was to move to New York City one day. "My entire goal from the eighth grade was to come here," she says. "To me it was everything they didn't have in Canton, Ohio, believe me! It was a good place to be from, but I wanted more. When I graduated from Mount Holyoke College in 1957, I came directly here. I roomed with three girls, all classmates from college, and our apartment was at 12 Fifth Avenue."

Colt met her future husband her very first night in New York and, two years later, married him. As newlyweds, they purchased a house on Horatio Street for $37,000 and moved in on November 6, 1959. "My mother-in-law was appalled," says Colt, laughing. "The West Village at that time was NOT the MacDougal-Sullivan Gardens, which is where she lived. Our house might as well have been in Siberia as far as she was concerned. It was quite an adventurous thing to do and everybody thought we were crazy."

What was Horatio Street like back then? "It was very working class and there was so much activity because of the Meat Market," Colt says. "In the middle of the block was a bodega. An Armenian woman owned it and lived in the back with her family. She cooked food and sold it to people who worked at the market. Because the kids who lived here were always outside, at the end of every weekend the entire street would be littered with Twinkie wrappers and soda pop bottles. And, of course, we had the railroad tracks that went through what is now 95 Horatio. At three o'clock in the morning those tracks would start switching and clanking and, God, the noise they made was amazing!"

"The houses on my side of the street were always nice, though," she continues. "And after a while, others started buying them. Then numbers 75 and 77 became the Masters Children Center, one of the first day care centers in New York City. And next door to me at number 81, before he went to Paris, you could see James Baldwin smoking on his balcony."

Colt began running her B&B in 1992 after her kids were grown and she needed to make money. What was it like having paying guests? "It was fun!" she readily admits. "In 22 years I had four people who were a problem. Maximum. Financially, it was very good to me as well, I must say. It allowed me to keep my house, which I couldn't have otherwise. It was only in the last few years that it didn't make enough money and that's when I decided to sell."

Besides, things had changed dramatically since Colt moved to Horatio Street. "It's just not my Village anymore," she says. "The people who moved into the house next to mine are so rich they installed a swimming pool in the back yard. It looks like a huge bathtub! That's when I thought, 'I've got to get out of here. I can't take it anymore.'" She finds it easier to leave, though, because of whom she sold her house to. "I didn't want to sell my house to some absentee oligarch who was going to come on a weekend every four or five months," Colt says. "Instead, I found a family with three young children who will have all my children's bedrooms. I'm so happy about that."

And yet after 55 years as a resident of the West Village, Colt admits she will miss the rhythm of life here. "It's going to be very hard not to walk to Jackson Square Pharmacy where everybody says, 'Hello, Mrs. Colt'", she says. "Or not to go to the bank where everybody greets me by name; or not to walk to Faicco's to get sausages." Then Colt stops to reflect for a moment. "But everybody that walks down Horatio Street is literally a stranger now. That didn't used to be the case. In fact, I spent a lot of time on my front stoop talking to my neighbors. In comparison, it's a very different life out here in California, but I think I'm ready for it."

West Village Original • Visual Arts

Elliott Gilbert

January 2013

Painter Elliott Gilbert was born in Brooklyn in 1924. After leaving the advertising profession in the early 1980s, Gilbert began to paint seriously, eventually spending summers in a monastery in Provence, France where he practiced his art. He and his wife were residents of St. Luke's Place for 49 years until moving to Hoboken last year.

In 1959, Elliott Gilbert found himself aboard the liner *SS Liberté*, bound for France and the life of an artist. Or so he thought. After meeting his future wife, Judith, on the boat and spending time in France "taking notes and making sketches," he returned to the USA. "I had to make a living before I could become an artist!" he says, chuckling. So he began working as an art director for BBDO, and ultimately went on to open his own ad agency. "However, I was always planning to leave at some point," he admits.

By the 1980s, Gilbert had become disillusioned enough with the advertising business that he seized his chance. "The business started to seem rather shallow to me," he says. "I just felt I wasn't getting anywhere so I sold my agency. That's when I really started painting and I got quite serious about it. It wasn't easy, either, because I had no contacts. But I entered competitions, joined art societies, peddled my paintings to galleries, and got my name out there. Eventually, I felt that the painting I was doing was pretty well appreciated all around." It was a good thing, too, because it turns out the life suits him. "I still feel more comfortable in expressing myself with painting than anything else," he says. "I paint in oils, watercolors, and pastels and it's a feeling of relief to be able to paint. Painting is my comfort and solace."

How does he determine what medium to work in? "That's a good question," he replies. "The watercolors are more spontaneous for me.

I'm able to work in them and immediately determine whether I like it or not. It's not as laborious as oils. With an oil painting it takes quite a long time for me to determine whether I was successful in what I was trying to do. It's a slower medium." Regardless of which medium Gilbert works in, he tries to convey his impressions of a scene rather than as an ultra-realistic rendition. "I really like to interpret what I see in an impressionistic manner. One thing I never wanted to do was be a slave to an image. I want it to be a point of departure and let my mind take over. That's why I like painting nature because I enjoy interpreting the light and dark aspects of what I see. Light has always been very important to me."

One of Gilbert's series is of the beautiful gardens at St. Luke's Church on Hudson Street. "The gardens were almost like a sanctuary what with the foliage and the trees. People would go in there as an escape from the hurly-burly of the city itself. I've done about fifteen paintings of the gardens—some in oil and some in watercolors—and those will be shown at the Hudson Park Library as part of my show."

Sadly, after living on St Luke's Place since 1963 and raising three sons there, Gilbert and his wife were suddenly forced to move last year when their building was sold. "It was almost a shock when it happened," Gilbert admits. "We didn't even have much time to move. We wanted very much to stay in the Village but we simply could not afford it now. It's become very, very chic and very expensive. It's almost a heartbreaker to see what's going on there." They ended up moving to Hoboken near one of their sons where they found the space they felt they needed. Still, the experience of living in this neighborhood will always be with them.

"The West Village was a major part of our lives," Gilbert says. "As an artist, the serenity of this area helped me very much. It was a very idyllic way to live because I had proximity to all of the city's activities yet I could come back to the Village where it was peaceful. To me it was the perfect spot. Forty-nine years is a long time to live in an area and then have to leave. And while my family and I left a lot of emotions and memories on St. Luke's Place, they're never going to leave us."

West Village Original • Visual Arts

Stephen Hall
March 2020

Painter Stephen Hall was born in Aberdeen, Scotland in 1954. A resident of Westbeth, Hall has exhibited throughout the U.S., India, Japan, Korea, and Mexico. His work is part of numerous corporate and private collections and has been featured in major motion pictures, music videos, and magazines.

"I always had this drive to draw and paint," says artist Stephen Hall. "I was never not doing that. According to my mother I was drawing behind the couch by the age of three or four. And I'm completely self-taught. I was actually very lucky, as well. I grew up in a council estate but thanks to the Eleven-plus exams, I was taken out of my working class school and sent to Aberdeen Grammar School, founded in the 14th Century. I was always a bit of a maverick, even back then, but the art teachers at the school were very encouraging to me. And my parents were always very supportive."

Hall admits that he didn't really become an artist until moving to New York in 1978. That was after hitchhiking around the world when he was about 19 and deciding he didn't want to return home. "I had seen a lot of the world and Aberdeen was too small a town for me," he says. "No offense to small towns, but I was looking for more. At one point I was working on a kibbutz in Israel. While I was there, I met a girl from New York and I came back with her and I eventually started exhibiting and selling my work. I've been here ever since."

What is Hall's preferred medium? "Acrylics," he answers. "They're the easiest and cleanest for me. I never had the patience for oil, the drying times. I believe, especially now, that oil is just a vehicle to move the pigments. And with acrylic you can make just as superior a painting as the classic oil painting. As far as my style goes, I think there's always been a recognizable vocabulary as being mine: a crisp color sense and graphic skill."

"I'm endeavoring to be more specific and less ambiguous in my work," he continues. "I still want to make beautiful, well-crafted paintings that aren't elitist and stimulate thinking. With my new series called *Earth Matters*—prompted by climate change—I'm fully up to my eyes in three-dimensional backgrounds of plastic, garbage, and rising sea levels. They get more and more complicated and harder to do. I often wish I was an Abstract Expressionist and could just throw paint on the canvas!" He laughs. "My paintings are meticulous and time-consuming. But doing the work is what drives me. Quite literally, the time I'm not painting is when I catch the flu or a cold. My resistance drops and my energy level drops. That's because I'm driven to paint. I've got no choice."

What has the life of an artist been like for Hall? "It's been like a wave that ebbs and flows," he says. "I've had times of great success and having patrons, and times when I didn't sell much work. I never became superfamous—although I was big in Japan at one point—but I do sell all my work." And as an artist, living in Westbeth has proven to be a "fantastic haven" for Hall as well. "Westbeth was set up to provide support for artists and it actually does that", he says. "For the 22 years I've been here it has seen me through some lean times. A lot of artists have had to move out of the city or get a corporate job, but I haven't due to the support of Westbeth."

The neighborhood has certainly changed, though. "There used to be transvestite hookers outside the building here," Hall says. "It was very cinematic. I enjoyed it. It's a bit more shopping mall now but I appreciate that since I have a thirteen-year old daughter who's always coming and going. Years ago, I had the good fortune to move to Bleecker Street between Charles and Tenth. It was my first apartment in the West Village and I fell in love with it. It was like a village. The streets weren't gridded, there was still a hint of Bohemia, and it was pretty and quiet. When we lost that apartment and moved to the East Village, I loved that too. It was raw, gritty, and arty. But when I had the opportunity to move into WestBeth and back to the West Village, I jumped at it. It was like coming home."

West Village Original • Visual Arts

Peter Harvey

May 2015

Painter and designer Peter Harvey was born in Guatemala in 1933 of British parents. He was a scenic designer for many years, working on both Broadway and Off-Broadway, as well as designing the original 1967 production of Balanchine's "Jewels" and the 2004 revival. Nowadays, Harvey devotes his time exclusively to painting—in both oil and watercolors—in the United States and France.

After a long and successful career as a theatrical set designer, Peter Harvey finally decided to call it quits in 1987. "I'd had it!" he says. "I went into the theatre because I felt it was an art and one that I loved. However, the love affair was over. After 30 years I found that here in New York it was a very commercial endeavor and nobody really cared if it was art. They wanted the easiest and cheapest thing on stage that they could get. Someone once suggested my name to a successful director and he responded, 'I don't want to use Peter. He's too creative.'" He laughs. "That's a great compliment, but it didn't get me the job!"

Besides, it was painting that always gave Harvey the greatest pleasure and continues to do so. It began when he first went to the University of Miami in Coral Gables. "In those days they were pushing abstract expressionism but I just couldn't get with that," he says. "I don't know why! I just couldn't think in those terms. You could get a nice effect and pretty colors but I never got any meaning out of it. Perhaps it's because I grew up in an earlier era and in an English environment. The children's books I had were illustrated with naturalistic, imaginative, and painterly images. I guess they had a profound effect on me."

What is it that he likes most about painting? "I love both the physical and emotional aspect," Harvey says. "When I'm done I feel at ease, rested, and complete, not at all worried and neurotic. It's cathartic."

One of his most creative periods was during the AIDS crisis while he was looking after a sick friend. "Robert and I had been partners and friends for 21 years," he says. "It's kind of funny and odd and sad to say, but those were the most creative years that I had. I worked all the time and nothing interrupted me. Robert didn't trouble me at all. There was no medication in those days but he was very strong and brave through it all. And, of course, it had an effect on me so I did paintings of him. After he died I did a big painting of him on his bed with his oxygen mask. I think it's the best one I've ever done."

Although he was a frequent visitor to New York before settling here, it was in 1958 that Harvey finally moved into the apartment he still lives in on Perry Street. What was it like to be a gay man in New York those days? "I didn't find it any problem at all," he says. "I was not tormented about being gay and once I made up my mind, it was very easy to find mutual friends and people who were interested in the same thing. There were bars throughout the city, so there was plenty of opportunity to meet others. You couldn't kiss and hold hands on the street like they do nowadays, but there were no problems. Some people may have found it difficult, but I think it depends on how quickly you accept yourself."

As for the West Village back then, Harvey claims that it was a real neighborhood. "There were funny little curiosity shops on Bleecker Street because you could rent a store for nothing," he recalls. "Early in the mornings you could hear the clinking of milk bottles being delivered to the apartment houses. My building was heated by coal and every few months the coal would rattle down the chute into the cellar. And while the streets are full of trees, many of them were only planted in the 1970s. I remember thinking I would never see them full-size!"

"Now I'm disappointed that it's become so high and mighty," he continues. "It's not a neighborhood anymore. It's full of tourists. Plus it's full of nannies pushing baby carriages. The new residents are such a fecund bunch! I can't disapprove of it, though, because all of New York has changed." Then Harvey pauses for a moment and has to admit that he still wouldn't want to live anywhere else. "It's still the Village," he says. "And you love it because you can see the sky."

West Village Original • Visual Arts

Rick Meyerowitz

September 2010

Illustrator, photographer, and writer Rick Meyerowitz was born in the Bronx in 1943. He spent twenty years with the National Lampoon as one of its most prolific contributors of illustrated articles. Abrams recently published his illustrated history of the magazine titled "DRUNK STONED BRILLIANT DEAD: The Writers and Artists Who Made the National Lampoon So Insanely Great."

Photo: Elizabeth Beautyman

For illustrator Rick Meyerowitz, early influences were not comic books as one might expect, but rather the notion of art itself. "My mother always took us to museums and exposed us to fine art," he recalls. "From my father, I got a love of drawing. While my influences were the great cartoonists and illustrators of my youth like N. C. Wyeth, Bill Mauldin, and David Low in England, I was also a great fan very early on of Jackson Pollack. I thought Willem de Kooning was the coolest stuff. I wanted to be an artist, but one who illustrated stories. So it wasn't comic books that influenced me so much as the idea that drawing pictures was something I could do which would give me pleasure."

After earning his degree from Boston University's School of the Arts, Meyerowitz returned to New York to begin his career as an illustrator. It was while delivering one of his illustrations to a client that his association with the *National Lampoon* began. "I ran into a writer named Michael O'Donoghue," he recalls. "He was a great, amazing, funny guy and we became friends. In September of 1969 he called me and said he would like me to meet a couple of guys from Harvard who were about to start a national humor magazine. We were introduced and I came on board to work with the *Lampoon* six months before they published their first issue. I like to say I'm an 'Original Lampooner.' I really was present at the birth."

As Meyerowtiz explains it, everyone was offended by the *Lampoon's* stick-in-your-eye style of humor. "The counter-culture thought that the magazine was on their side," he says. "They asked, 'How could you attack Joan Baez or Bob Dylan? We thought you were with us!' But we weren't on anybody's side. As far as we were concerned, they were as pathetic a target as the Nixon administration or Pat Boone. For myself, I wasn't interested in offending anybody. I was just against hypocrisy and deadly dullness. To me, the lunatic actions of the Left were as crazy as the lunatic actions of the Right."

"Although I had a huge impact on the look of the *Lampoon* for all those years," he continues, "I also had another life." This included raising two children, living on Jane Street for many years and then moving to Charles Street, where he still resides. "All the while that was going on," he says, "I was illustrating about 2000 ads for advertising agencies and articles for other magazines. The *Lampoon* was just a small part of my income and a small part of my production."

When Meyerowitz and his family moved here in early 1977, "It was really great," he remembers. "I would play stickball with my son on Greenwich Street and a car would come by every twenty minutes. The streets were that empty. Ours was one of the first conversions of an industrial building and that was pretty extraordinary at the time."

While he is bemused by the significant changes to the West Village since, Meyerowitz is not a fan of preserving it in amber, either. "I don't think the area should be locked in time or stay exactly the same," he admits. "While I love the historic and low-rise character of this neighborhood, I am somewhat tired of derivative red-brick buildings being built to look like something old. I believe you can retain the character of this neighborhood and still have some interesting and forward-looking architecture."

What never changes for Meyerowitz, though, is his sense of having found a home in the West Village. "What I love is the light and the air and how I feel when I return from being uptown," he says. "There's a sense of relief to be in the quiet, sunny streets. It's a small town thing and it always gives me a sense of homecoming. I know these streets very well. I'm often amused when I see people on all four corners studying maps, trying to figure out where the hell they are. The question is, do I help any of them or just smile and go home?" Then he says, laughing, "Because I know where I am and they don't!"

West Village Original • Visual Arts

Kika Schoenfeld

April 2011

Photo: Kika Schoenfeld

Kika Schoenfeld is artist, interior designer, and hat designer. As an interior designer her work includes the Getty Museum in Los Angeles. As a hat designer, her one-of-a-kind pieces can be found here in New York at the Cooper Hewitt and Moss, as well as in shops in London, Tokyo, and online.

For artist and designer Kika Schoenfeld, except for the occasional foray to spend a few years in Los Angeles or Greece, her entire adult life has been centered on New York's Greenwich Village. "I was born in Tel Aviv, and I came to New York at the age of eight with my parents," she says. "We first lived in a hotel in the Upper West Side and then I grew up in Riverdale. When I became an adult I went to Cooper Union, so I was luckily and happily introduced by definition to the lower Village area. Over the years I continued to move further and further west. Now I'm in the West Village and have been for the past two decades."

"After I gradated from Cooper I decided to embark on the life of an artist, so to speak," she continues. "I got married and had a child, and my husband supported my painting. Then we got divorced and I had to support myself. I wasn't able to do it from painting alone and decided to consider going into architecture. In addition to painting, I had studied architecture with Richard Meier at Cooper Union so one night I contacted him to ask his advice. He suggested that I simply go into the world as an interior designer and learn the trade as I went along." That is, indeed, what Schoenfeld did; and she found some wonderful opportunities along the way, including moving to Los Angeles for three years to work with Meier designing the Getty.

It was while back in the city that the "big crash" of 2008 forced

Schoenfeld to find alternative ways to earn a living. "Suddenly, my interior design work was down to zero," she says. "I had time on my hands and needed to figure out a way to make money. So I thought I would knit. I had enjoyed doing it as a girl and I always found knitting a very meditative process. I could really think things out while doing it."

After some trial and error—and deciding slippers and gloves were too troublesome because "I had to make two of them and they had to match!"—Schoenfeld learned the technique of felting. "The fascinating thing is that after knitting and boiling the wool, it comes out different every time," she says. "It's always a bit of a surprise for me, which I love. Otherwise it would get boring." And even though her business is expanding in gratifying ways, Schoenfeld still does all the hats herself. "Each one is numbered and each one is in one way or another unique," she says.

As a resident of the West Village for many years, Schoenfeld has a unique perspective on the change that has come to the neighborhood. "Actually, it's what I would call the 'awakening' of the West Village," she says. "It used to be sleepy and quiet and it was wonderful for that. It had its little shops, ethnic bakeries, and butchers, particularly around Bleecker Street. Now there's Marc Jacobs and Ralph Lauren and the like. So it's as if it got polished up. However, even as Bleecker has become ritzier, I find the side streets have stayed completely wonderful. So I'm hoping it's possible to keep things naturally contained like that."

Schoenfeld also speaks excitedly about what is happening in the formerly industrial Meat Market area. "Personally, I'm delighted with additions like the High Line, as well as all the new architecture that's going up in the far West Village. I think it's wonderful and exciting and beautiful and not deadly. As long as it doesn't spread into—and spoil—the rest of the Village!"

For Schoenfeld, spending a creative lifetime here has almost been a blessing. "To me it's the heart of the heart of the heart of the country," she confesses. "That's it. It's like ground zero for life. If you're going to live in this world at this time, the West Village is probably one of the loveliest places to be if you're going to be in a city. If you live a life like I do, where I shuttle between my house on the North Fork with its solitude and the West Village, it's the best combination there is. I'm really lucky to have it."

West Village Original • Visual Arts

Jenny Tango
November 2018

Photo: Robert Bunkin

Artist Jenny Tango was born Florence Exler in Brooklyn in 1926. A visual artist working collaboratively and individually in painting, communications media, artist's books and comic strips, Tango received both a BA and MA from Brooklyn College. With a list of both solo and group exhibitions to her name, Tango lives in Westbeth with her husband, artist Robert Bunkin.

"I had the most wonderful parents in the world," Jenny Tango confesses. "I now realize they weren't perfect, but I grew up thinking they were! My father worked in the garment industry and my mother was a housewife, but there was also an artistic aspect in the family. So, I had a cultured background even though we were working class."

As a young girl, Tango was lucky enough to attend the new High School of Music and Art in New York. "I gravitated towards painting because I like to draw," she says. "Then at Brooklyn College I ended up in the painting program. That was the time that Abstract Expressionism came out and everybody had to paint like that. You couldn't do figures! After I graduated I tried Abstract Expressionism for two years and decided it was the most boring thing! So, I went back to figurative painting because there was so much to learn."

What does Tango like best about painting? "It gives me the opportunity to look," she replies. "I love looking! Looking to me is an adventure because when you stop and look you discover things. And you never know where it's going to take you. But looking is different than seeing. Seeing gives you the end results: 'I see this. I see that.' Whereas looking is a process of discovery, and that's what makes life so exciting."

Did Tango face any resistance because of her gender in the art world? "It was difficult being a woman artist back then," she says.

"When I returned to Brooklyn College in 1960 for my masters, I was asked to teach a course in art education. Well, that upset the entire male art department! I guess a woman seemed dangerous. The next year I was given a teaching fellowship and a male classmate received the office fellowship, which was usually given to a woman. However, when we graduated he got a job teaching there and I didn't!"

For personal reasons, this turned out to be "the best thing" that happened to Tango. "I ended up teaching in high school where I met my husband, Robert. He was a student in my class and we became close. He was very bright, talented, saw me as a painter and wanted me to go back to it. When I met him, I was happily married with two children. I had to make a very difficult decision. So, even though there's a 28-year difference between us, I married him. This was during the 60s, an incredible period of creation in the arts. Robert and I were both artists in a world that was bursting with new ideas, and it was just fabulous."

Interestingly enough, as much as she loved the Village, Tango didn't move here until 2014. Why did she finally do it? "Because it was a dream I had since I was 16 and first discovered it," she replies. "I was determined to do it before I died. Robert and I were living on Staten Island when I put in an application to Westbeth. Well, 24 years went by when I suddenly got this notice that an apartment was available. I said, 'Are you waiting until you have to bring me there in a box?' I was 88!"

"So, we moved to Westbeth," she continues. "We gave up two floors in a house on Staten Island for an apartment that's as big as our old kitchen was. We got rid of everything we owned. It's a small space in which we both paint as well, but we're so involved in our art that we're happy." When asked if she and her husband still get along in such close quarters, Tango laughs. "What keeps us together is art," she says. "It doesn't matter where we are."

The Village of her 16-year-old self, though, is quite different from today. "The art world is going like the Village," Tango says. "It's just about money. People still come here from all over the world, but it's an illusion of what New York and the Village used to be. I had to deal with that when I moved here and I've come to terms with it. I realize that this isn't my world anymore, either. It's a world of young people. But we've been through this before and we will be through it again as long as there's an earth and a human race. We will have our ups and downs. We will be wonderful and we will be bad."

West Village Original • Visual Arts

Mary Vaccaro
November 2009

Artist Mary Vaccaro can regularly be seen painting on the streets of the neighborhood. Her meticulous, time-consuming paintings of the West Village contain both historical and religious aspects. A graduate of Cooper Union, Mary has lived for the past 25 years on Jane Street with her spouse, Christine. Her work can be seen at www.maryvaccaro.com.

For painter and sculptor Mary Vaccaro, drawing is something she has done since she was a child. "I always drew," she admits. "Constantly drew, painted, and built things. I always carried a book and drew on the subways. In high school I painted on the ceiling in my art class. I used those things to get into Cooper Union and I got right in. It was the only school I applied to."

Were her parents artists themselves? "No," she replies. "My father, who is from Staten Island, had an electrical company. He wired a lot of Staten Island when it was being built up. He also restores antique cars, which can take years. That's where I get my patience. My grandfather Vaccaro did paint for himself, but for work he put marble in buildings, including the Chrysler Building."

According to Vaccaro, Staten Island was still rural when she was growing up there and traveling into Manhattan was going into the "big city." "When I was in high school," she recalls, "I would come into New York almost every weekend; sometimes with friends, sometimes by myself. One weekend we'd go to the 57th Street galleries and another we'd spend in Soho. We'd go to the Met or the Whitney or the Guggenheim. That's how I learned about art. I looked at everything and I liked everything: the Cloisters, Russian art, new art, old art."

So how did she come to paint street views? "It started when I had a job on Fifth Avenue and 30th Street," she remembers. "My boss asked me to paint his view, which I did. Then my father said, 'Why don't you paint the view from your own window?' So I painted my view of Jane Street, with the garage and a corner of the Guerin building. At that time the garage had broken windows and a lot of graffiti. It wasn't as pretty as it is now. That was my first historical painting of the Village."

In doing so, Vaccaro's intentions were twofold: to document what was truly there by not "prettying it up" and to add the kind of symbolism that painters of the past would. "Artists used to paint for either donors or churches and insert a story into the painting, such as a moral tale," she explains. "I try to put those aspects in my paintings as well. You can walk through them, so to speak, and experience different things."

Talking about how the neighborhood has changed since she moved here in 1984, Vacarro recalls, "It was a bit rougher; never dangerous or bad, but a whole different character. Three times our car window was broken into when we parked it on the street. At that time, I worked for *Womenews* on far West 14th Street and that was a little dangerous coming home at night. Not only were the streets covered with gizzards and slimy leftovers from the meat market, but a lot of unsavory people hung around as well."

"Everything changes so fast in the Village these days", she continues. "I see people all day long on the corner when I paint. There's still plenty of free spirits in the West Village but there's also a lot of fancy people as well. They head to the meatpacking district. I can't say it's one hundred percent a good thing but I also can't say all progress is a bad thing either." At the end of the day, though, Vaccaro wouldn't live anywhere else. "I'm so lucky to be here," she says. "For one thing, this neighborhood has great transportation and subway access. Granted, we've lost a lot of little shops, but I still love it."

For Vaccaro, the vibrancy of the West Village lies not only in painting outdoors, but in the interactions with her neighbors as well. "It takes me a couple of years to do one painting," she confesses. "Partly because I just keep going over and over the same things—which is how the details come out—and partly because I say hello to anybody who stops to chat. People have a lot to say and they become part of the whole process. It's the people that really get me on the street. It's great to be out, to be part of the West Village, and to be part of the flow of things."

> *I've been delighted and privileged to be here. In the final analysis, I think what the Village always represented to me was a sense of possibility, and that's still here.*
>
> —John Tytell

West 12th Street

West Village Original • Writing

Nancy Bogen

August 2011

Photo: Nancy Bogen

Writer and photographer Nancy Bogen was born in Brooklyn in 1932. For thirty years she taught English Lit at Richmond College and the College of Staten Island, retiring as professor emeritus in 1997. The author of three novels, including "Klytaimnestra Who Stayed at Home," as well as a photographer, she lives with her husband, Arnold, on Jane Street.

"I'm no normal 79-year-old," boasts writer and photographer Nancy Bogen. "I run about two miles every day. I also engage in sports. I play ping pong, and I used to fence at the Salle Santelli on Sixth Avenue. It's not only for my health that I exercise, but for my frame of mind as well. I think it keeps me rather sane, for one. It keeps the cobwebs away."

It's this kind of energy that has seen the longtime West Villager through a number of careers, beginning with one as a writer. "My parents were not professional writers, but they wrote well. I remember as a little girl I went to public school in Brooklyn and I had a teacher who was a real meanie. It took a lot impress her, but she once looked at me and said, 'You know, you can write!' That was the beginning of my career," she says, laughing.

As an adult, Bogen went on to write three novels of ideas and many scholarly articles. Eventually the late John Gardner, the best-selling author of novels such as *The Sunlight Dialogues*, befriended her. "He loved my first novel and went to bat for it," she recalls. "He was advising me about what would become my third novel when he was killed in a motorcycle accident. That was devastating to me." At the same time, Bogen's serious fiction writing all went—according to her—"down hill." "That's because the kind of novel I was writing— the novel of ideas that required full attention—began to lose its audience," she says. "And even though they loved my writing, my agents couldn't place my work anymore." For Bogen, this was a harbinger of the current lamentable state of literature. "Nobody reads serious fiction any more!" she says. "It's gone, it's finished, the art of reading. Ask young people if they've read *Ulysses,* or anything by William Faulkner. Thomas Wolfe is a complete unknown. It can be very depressing if you let it get to you."

Bogen shifted gears when she retired from teaching in 1997 and founded a small performance group called The Lark Ascending. "I always loved music, and my mission was to create performances that included both that and literature, related by scene or period," she explains. "I would commission an 8–10 minute piece by a living composer. I felt that composers had no one to speak for them. The music is there in notes on paper but if they don't get a performance, no one hears it."

Throughout it all, Bogen was an avid photographer. "I started out as a writer but I always wanted to be a photographer," she admits. "Once I was established in a teaching career with a regular income I began doing photography, very modestly at first, and then more and more. But I found shooting film very limiting, and when digital imaging came along I really felt that I came into my own. It's all come together. I'm now finding myself as both a writer and digital imagist and putting it with text and music on Vimeo."

A West Village resident since 1971, Bogen had her first one-person show as a photographer right here on Bleecker Street. In recollecting it, she tells the kind of story that for her could only happen in the Village. "I had been homebound for three months with a hurt back," she says. "The doctor said I could get up for only ten minutes a day. So for those ten minutes, I shot pictures from my apartment window. I shot whatever went by: balloons, helicopters, clouds, you name it. Afterwards, I went to the 380 Gallery and told the owner that this was how I happened to take the pictures. He took one look and said, 'I'm going to give you a show.'"

"I was an unknown!" she continues. "An utter stranger. I never had anything happen like that anywhere else in New York. But that was the kind of thing that could happen here in the Village, which is why I love it."

West Village Original • Writing

Susan Brownmiller

April 2010

Born in Brooklyn in 1935, writer and feminist Susan Brownmiller's groundbreaking book, "Against Our Will," was published in 1975 and changed forever the way society looks at rape. Since then she has written–among other things– "In Our Time," a memoir of the feminist revolution, and the novel "Waverly Place." These days Ms. Brownmiller teaches travel writing at NYU and women's studies at Pace.

For Susan Brownmiller, childhood nurturing by both her family and schools provided a foundation that still supports her. "My parents truly appreciated the arts and culture," she recalls. "I was taken to plays, dance recitals, and concerts. There were always books and newspapers in our home. And Franklin D. Roosevelt was king in our house! In addition, I went to schools that actually encouraged writing. It's amazing in light of what you read about the state of schools today, but in our little part of Brooklyn there was a lot of attention paid to writing and to literature."

After graduating from Cornell, Brownmiller first moved to New York to be an actor. "While studying acting," she says, "I accidentally fell into editorial-type jobs for magazines and learned some skills." Her writing career actually started in Mississippi. "I went there in the summer of 1964 as a volunteer to work in the civil rights movement," she says. "In fact, I wrote my first piece for the *Village Voice* from Mississippi. It was a momentous summer for the nation, as well as for myself. But my whole life I've always asked myself, 'Am I an activist, am I a writer, am I a hopeful actor?' I was very lucky when the women's movement came along because I could combine my activism with writing."

It was being inside this movement that changed Brownmiller's mind about rape and prompted her to write *Against Our Will*. "I had grown up with the misconception liberals held that no woman could be raped against her will," she says. "But a new movement surfaced that had rediscovered rape and took it out of the dark ages. What had been missing was the voice of women who actually experienced rape and how they felt during it, the fear that they could possibly die. Before that, nobody had elicited any great body of information from women themselves. Then it dawned on people that we weren't talking about the defendants, but about the victims." *Against Our Will* became a seminal work in its field, and in 1995 the New York Public Library declared it one of 100 most important books of the 20th century. After its publication, Brownmiller spent the next two years lecturing about rape at colleges and universities across the country. More importantly, "I watched the nation's laws on sexual assault change to reflect a victim's understanding of the crime," she says.

Brownmiller moved to the West Village in 1966, prompted by a desire to recapture the charm of Center City, Philadelphia where she had once briefly lived. "When I first moved here to Jane Street, nobody wanted to live this far west," she says, laughing. "I remember when Hudson Street was filled with furniture stripping places. I remember when the Meatpacking district was absolutely thriving, but as an industrial area. I remember the frankfurter factory on the corner of Jane and Greenwich Streets and the ice cream factory on Jane Street. And there was the smell of ink from the Superior Inks factory down by the river."

And how has it changed? "Suddenly, I'm living on the edge of a very trendy neighborhood of restaurants and clubs," Brownmiller observes. "The character of people has changed, too. It seems to me we used to have people with less money but with more commitment to art and writing. And the whole concept of the local neighborhood restaurant is gone from the West Village!" The pace of change here can be startling as well, she admits. "When I walk around, I find myself saying, 'When did this restaurant or business close and when did this one open?' She laughs. "It's like a travel experience!"

Brownmiller does see things stabilizing at some point, though. "We're going through a period that's unstable because businesses open and close so much," she says. "But I think this time will pass. It will stabilize. I think it has to stabilize and we'll move back to a more friendly neighborhood and one not so concerned with attracting a trendy crowd. That crowd never stays in one place for long, anyway."

West Village Original • Writing

Jack Dowling
April 2016

Painter and writer John (Jack) Dowling was born in Woodbridge, New Jersey in 1931. After attending Cooper Union and teaching in Italy for a few years, he settled in New York to be a painter before eventually turning to writing. His stories have been published in the Hamilton Stone Review, the Barcelona Review, A&U Magazine, and American Writing. He has been a resident of WestBeth since 1971.

Jack Dowling spent the first two decades of his life in New York City as a painter. "There were centers of activity in the Village and I just quietly began to paint," he says. "At some point I gave up painting abstractly because I wasn't sure where that was going. One day, I picked up a snapshot of my parents on their wedding day and decided to make a painting from that. I developed that into a kind of semi-abstraction and got very involved in the sense of light, color, and shadow. That resulted in a whole series of paintings that had their initial source in photographs."

What made him stop painting and take up writing? "It sounds like a sob story," he says, laughing. "I had a large loft and I got involved in a court case trying to save it. It cost me money that I didn't have, which sent me into the job market and diverted me from my painting. After three years, I lost the loft and I was homeless at 40!" He laughs. "But I got myself reorganized and into WestBeth in a 'starter' apartment. I was still working at the job that I had gotten to survive but I had also decided I didn't want to paint anymore. In the meantime I began to jot down various short observations and channel my creative energy in that direction."

Does he find writing different than painting? "Writing is very creative, but it's ten times harder than painting was for me," Dowling admits. "I worked really hard because in the beginning I couldn't write anything more than a big paragraph. I still have to write and rewrite because I don't have an easy time constructing a story that is grammatically proper. At the same time, I don't want to make it so correct that it loses its punch. So it took me a number of years to figure out how to write my stories."

Having lived in New York since the early 1950s, Dowling has spent most of those years in the neighborhood. "You could move around back then. You'd move into an apartment with your suitcase and maybe your cat on your shoulder. And then you'd hear about a nicer apartment somewhere else and you'd pick up and move. That was what the Village was like." There was also a lively gay scene. "There were three gay bars on 8th Street back in the 50s," he recalls. "There was Mary's, the Colony which was also a restaurant, and then a place called Main Street. For a gay man, the Village was a comfortable, easy kind of place. I never felt like an outsider even when I was younger."

By the 1970s, though, the Village was a "mess" as was the whole City. "When Westbeth first opened it was so gritty and grimy down here, still a factory neighborhood. It was not high-end by any means. Now there's a ton of money in the Village! I saw a reference to 10014 as one of the zip codes with the highest incomes in NYC. But those of us in WestBeth wouldn't know about that," he says laughingly.

"However, I love living here," he continues. "Considering what's become of New York, I feel fortunate to still be here and in WestBeth, which is like living in a small town. People are coming and going all day long, working on their creative projects. It's not like other apartment buildings here in the neighborhood that are dormant all day long; we're a thriving, energetic jewel right in the middle of what's become a rather boring neighborhood."

When asked what it is about the artistic process that initially attracted him, Dowling responds, "For myself, I feel I was born with it. Never for a moment did I consider following in my businessman father's footsteps. Instead, I was always thinking about stuff to make. That's a good part of it. There are a lot of people in creative fields who didn't have a choice. We're just drawn into it and we can't resist it."

West Village Original • Writing

John Gilman
January 2020

Photo: George Bonanno

Author and journalist John Gilman was born in Honolulu, Hawaii. With his life partner Robert Heide, Gilman began writing the two-page centerfold for the Village Voice in the 1970s and, one thing leading to another, ended up as co-author of many pop culture books that focused on the Depression and Mickey Mouse. Gilman has also written a number of guidebooks with Heide.

For author John Gilman, born in Hawaii, it turned out that his father's profession would eventually become his as well. "My father was a well-known and well-regarded newspaperman," he says. "He was in Shanghai writing about China for the International News Service when the Japanese starting bombing them. So he and my mother went to Hawaii, where he wrote for *The Honolulu Advertiser*. And they were there when the Japanese bombed Pearl Harbor!" This time the family stayed for quite some time. "I spent my first seven years on the beach at Waikiki where I swam before I walked."

After the war, Gilman, along with his mother and brother, took a ship to San Francisco where John went to school, all the way from grammar school through college. "After that, I started taking trips to New York City where I would live for a while and then go back to San Francisco," he says. "Finally, one day I was standing in Sheridan Square and made the decision to settle here for good. So I moved to the Village, met playwright Robert Heide at the Caffe Cino, and we became a couple. That was 1965."

It was Gilman's love of collecting "the things that nobody else wanted" that led to a string of books. "My being from California meant that Bob and I had a car in New York," he says. "So we hit the highways, mostly in New Jersey, combing the flea markets and antique centers. Eventually the stuff we bought told us the story of the

Depression. It was kind of a 'made in America' story because everything was made in America back then. That informed our first book, *Dime-Store Dream Parade,* which was about popular culture. Then we realized you're only as good as your last book, so we did another one and then another. Along the way we acquired an agent and by the time we finished we had written fifteen books together. At the same time, we were doing magazine and newspaper articles as well. We were busy!"

"When I say 'we' I mean our bylines," Gilman continues. "We stuck with Robert Heide first because he had a very good touch in terms of his writing. They were nonfiction books, but Bob brought a human element to them. I was a wiz at gathering the facts, so while our books were fun to read, they were also good references for the period they were covering."

What appealed to Gilman most about his research? "We discovered that in the 1930s every company hired industrial designers to redesign their products in a streamlined, modern style, using new materials such as plastic," he says. "Our books are about how those new products were merchandised—the way America pulled up its boots straps by merchandising everything in a positive, can-do way. We looked at the cheerful side of the Depression, if you will. We covered the dark side, too, but what we tried to do was emphasize the good parts. We discovered it was a very creative and upbeat decade."

When Gilman moved to New York in 1965, some vestiges of an earlier time still existed. "I remember very clearly when the cobblestones on Seventh Avenue were replaced by macadam," he says. "I came out one day and the cars were whizzing by at a frightful speed. That was a big change! Bob and I miss the many coffee houses and the laid back, slow pace of the Village that used to be. But all of the amenities are at our fingertips here and it couldn't be a better place to live. I know it's crazy to say, but I think it's the best place in America to live."

Gilman also says he's been noticing lately that commercial rents seem to be coming down. "That's a good sign," he says. "After all those high-end shops paying enormous rents closed up and left Bleecker Street for dead, we now see pop-up shops filling the spaces. Maybe the future will be bright. I look on the bright side of things anyway." He laughs. "I've studied the Depression! If you were down in those days, you could go see a Busby Berkeley or a Mickey Mouse film. That's because you knew you had to keep smiling."

West Village Original • Writing

Catherine Revland

August 2018

Photo: Maggie Berkvist

Writer and author Catherine Revland was born in 1940 in Fort Ransom, North Dakota and raised in Fargo. Formally educated and trained as a writer, she has over 40 years experience writing for a variety of print and online media. Her current project is titled "What the Old Ones Knew: Communicating with the Ancestors," an oral history of the Yankton Sioux as told to Revland.

As a girl growing up in Fargo, North Dakota with a father who was ill for a time, writer Catherine Revland discovered the world of books. "I kind of escaped into books because my Dad was so sick," she says. "I got a prize for reading 100 books in the first grade. But that's not unusual. I think most writers were originally avid readers and kind of in love with what words do, or don't do for that matter. One day when I was 12, I discovered a book in the public library about a woman writer who lived in a place called Greenwich Village. I said to myself, 'That's it! That's what I want to be and where I want to live!'"

But first Revland had to finish school, attend the University of North Dakota on a journalism scholarship, get married, and have her first child. "Finally, in 1963, when I was seven months pregnant with our second daughter, my actor husband and I left Fargo for New York in a broken-down car and with no money," she says. "I worked as an actress and model until I got pregnant for the third time and then I had to make a decision. I gave up modeling and I started to work in book publishing, which eventually led to ghostwriting."

Revland attributes her success as a ghostwriter to the fact that she could put her ego in her back pocket. "A colleague once told me that I was so good at it because I know how to worm my way into a person's psyche but also when to pull back," she says. "It's a very intimate relationship being a ghostwriter. Someone will tell you things they never tell anyone else. They want the ghostwriter to tell the truth but also varnish it up a little bit. They want it to be their story, but they have to be careful about how they appear to the world when the book comes out."

Is ghost writing enough of a creative outlet, though? "No. You give up your creativity, actually," Revland admits. "It's very dependable work when you're raising kids and I was a single parent by that time. But after a while I realized I had to write my own books. And when I got into my own writing I wasn't a novice. I feel very grateful for all the ghost writing I did because of what I learned; particularly how to transmit the verbal into the written word."

After living in a "nice, quiet neighborhood in Brooklyn," Revland finally moved into the Village in an apartment at Tenth and Waverly. "It was a crappy apartment that cost $350 a month," she says. "But I was with my three daughters, a Belgian Shepherd, two cats, and we were just thrilled! I had waited a long time to fulfill my dream of living here. What's so great about being in one place for 40 years is that there's continuity. Every time I walk down these streets my life flashes before my eyes. All these things have happened to me in the Village and that's why it's so dear to me."

Does Revland regret how much the neighborhood has changed over her four decades here? "There's something so unproductive about mourning what's no longer there," she responds. "When I walk around the Village I see incredible ironwork, or beautiful doors, or streets that still have their cobblestones. There's so much here that hasn't changed thanks to historical preservation. And I try not to dwell on what has changed because I've changed too. There are parts of my life that I yearn for, but I also love what I'm doing right now. I wouldn't be young again for anything! Really. It's a waste of time, which is my most precious commodity right now. I still have things to do. I mean, I haven't been to Paris yet!" She laughs. "How can that be?!"

West Village Original • Writing

Barbara Riddle
December 2010

Author and WestView contributor Barbara Riddle was born in Wickersham Hospital on East 58th Street and grew up in an impressive number of different locations, all in the Village. The author of "The Girl Pretending to Read Rilke" she is currently living on West 12th Street and completing her memoir, "Sex and Sinclair Lewis: Tales of a Greenwich Village Girlhood."

For author Barbara Riddle, growing up in the bosom of Greenwich Village during the 1950's is the stuff of fond memories. "What I remember is the total freedom we had," she says. "We had no fears. My friends and I hung out in Washington Square Park every day. We'd talk, flirt with each other, ride bikes, and roller skate. We'd stay out late on summer nights. Back then, the Village was mostly Irish and Italian working class and crazy Bohemians, like my mother. She was a writer, raising me on her own, who always had very experimental tastes. She would take me to the 8th Street Playhouse to see foreign films, or to the Living Theater. She also had gay friends and interracial friends and I took for granted that that's how everybody was."

"My father was a weekend dad," she continues. "He would take me to MOMA and the original Whitney, which back then was on West 8th Street opposite the Hotel Marlton. Lots of interesting people lived in that hotel. In fact, my mother and I wound up there several times when she couldn't afford the rent and we got evicted from our latest apartment. My mother liked it because it was inexpensive and clean and there was always a clerk in the lobby who could babysit me. I didn't mind it because I was still able to go to PS 41. Another time we lived at the Hotel Albert on University and 10th, as well as the Hotel Earl, now the Washington Square Hotel."

According to Riddle, this itinerant upbringing is why she knows the

Village so well. "In addition to hotels, we lived on Charles Street, Perry Street, and then one time on Bank Street in a townhouse. When I would walk my younger sibling to school in the morning, we would pass these huge barrels of cow heads discarded by the butchers in the Meatpacking District. It looked like *Guernica* in a barrel," she says, laughing, "with the tongues sticking out and the eyeballs bulging."

When she was 16, Riddle left New York to attend Reed College. "I thought science was fantastic," she says. "But I was very conflicted because I also wanted to write. I did get my PhD in Biochemistry, but I turned down a postdoctoral fellowship to Oxford and moved to London with my partner instead." It turned out to be the right decision. "I kissed the ground every morning I woke up," she confesses. "And I did publish a novel, *The Girl Pretending to Read Rilke*. It's about a girl working in a science lab, and a lot of it is autobiographical." The experience was cathartic for Riddle. Through the novel she was able to come to terms with her father's suicide when she was eighteen. "It was very liberating to come to the understanding that a young woman cannot give meaning to her father's life," she says. "You never get over something like that, but you can separate it from personal guilt."

Riddle subsequently moved from London to San Francisco where she and her partner raised a daughter. "I never acclimated to San Francisco," she admits. "My heart was always in New York and I came back to the Village full-time in 2002." However, it was a very different neighborhood from the one she had left years before. "The biggest change is that it now takes a lot of money to live here," she observes. "That means that people are under more pressure. You can see that they don't have as much time to talk to each other or do unstructured things. I do lament the fact that people don't seem to have time to enjoy what we have here."

"Nevertheless," she continues, "I still think the Village is one of the most livable neighborhoods in this city. Physically, it doesn't look that different. If I squint, it could be the same as it was forty years ago." And writing for *WestView* has given back to Riddle a sense of community. "I was so happy to connect with the paper for that reason. It's the best of the old and the new. You have to move on, of course, and you can't recreate the past. But a lot of the people at *WestView* are managing to live in the present while maintaining the old Village values and to me that's a very successful combination."

West Village Original • Writing

Andrew Rubenfeld
May 2020

Editor, college professor, and avid bird watcher Andrew Rubenfeld was born in Beth Israel Hospital in 1946. Since 1981, he has been a professor of literature at Stevens Institute of Technology in New Jersey where he teaches courses on American nature and environmental writing. Rubenfeld co-edited "American Birds: A Literary Companion," published by the Library of America this March.

As a child growing up first in the Bronx and then the suburbs on Long Island, Andrew Rubenfeld was widely exposed to literature, music, and art. So when it came time to go to college, it was a bit of a surprise when his parents suggested he study chemistry. "I was good in chemistry and they wanted me to have a career," Rubenfeld says. "So I said 'Okay' and was accepted to Clark University. However, the summer before my freshman year they had orientation and we had to read Thoreau's *Walden* before we attended it. The book changed my life! I arrived at Clark as a chemistry major but never took a single chemistry course. Instead I became a literature major from day one. I just knew it was what I wanted to do. And that's how I really got connected with literature. I ended up doing my masters thesis on English Renaissance literature and my doctorate on Mark Twain at NYU."

And how did Rubenfeld discover bird watching? "It was in the early 1980s and my partner and I were at Acadia National Park in Maine. It was mid July and teeming with birds. It was also post breeding so it was full of young birds as well. The park ranger said those little birds were going to fly nonstop to Florida or even Venezuela. So we looked at them through our binoculars and the very next day bought a second pair. We redid the whole trip so we could look at birds. I suddenly had a passion."

"At some point I started becoming more and more aware of how much American nature writing there is," he continues. "It's an integral part of American literature, which includes Audubon, Emerson, Thoreau, and John Muir to name a few. So my teaching and birding just coalesced. This semester I'm teaching a course on Thoreau and American Nature and Environmental Writing. We focus mainly on his work titled *The Maine Woods,* published posthumously by his sister. It's a wonderful book. It shows him moving from nature writing to environmental writing as he's putting it all together. I love teaching, I love American literature, and I love looking at birds. All in all, I think that's a pretty wonderful combination."

Rubenfeld considered his efforts on *American Birds: A Literary Companion* to be "a labor of love." He had been a contributing editor at the Library of America for over twenty years and knew he wanted them to publish it. "When the topic came up someone asked me to put together a table of contents," he says. "I had it to them in a week because it was basically my teaching files from school. I'm very pleased with the final product. It's 300 pages and includes 75 authors. The Library of America is a not-for-profit publisher, so there are no royalties. It's just fee-for-hire and that's fine. I sometimes think of it as a gift to my friends and fellow bird watchers. It was a thoroughly enjoyable endeavor."

Rubenfeld always wanted to live in the West Village and by the mid-1970s he had accomplished that. "Nothing else even remotely seemed possible for me," he says. "It just felt right." And while much has changed, the spirit of the place has remained for him. "This neighborhood never lost that sense of being a little different, a little queer, a little off the wall, a little small-town. The people who moved here knew they were coming to the Village, not just some place in the City. I still get that sense today."

"I don't see the West Village becoming homogenized like any other neighborhood," he continues. "There are surface changes that reflect changes in American society and culture, but there's a core set of values that has a lot to do with independence as well as caring. We're all in it together. We're in this virus thing together. That aloof New York attitude is just a veneer, something we like to pretend we have. I think the essence of the Village is do your own stuff, it's none of my business, but if you need me, I'm available. I haven't seen that change and that's why I'm still here."

West Village Original • Writing

John Tytell
October 2010

Writer John Tytell's works on such literary figures as Jack Kerouac, Ezra Pound, Allen Ginsberg, Henry Miller, and William S. Burroughs have made him a leading scholar of the Beat Generation. His latest book is "Reading New York," a "hybrid memoir" of both growing up and reading in the City. A longtime professor at Queens College where he still teaches literature, Tytell and his wife, Mellon, moved to Perry Street in 1967.

Born into a family of diamond merchants in Antwerp, Belgium in 1939, John Tytell emigrated to America with them two years later and grew up on the Upper West Side. Afflicted with vernal catarrh until the age of 12, Tytell was warned that—because of sensitivity to light—reading would only strain his already compromised eyes. "As a kind of compensation I began reading by flashlight at night when no one knew," he recalls. "That experience of reading Melville and Poe—among others—gave me a sense of a great American literary tradition. That was one of the things that led me on the path that I later took."

That path was going to college to study history, philosophy, and, ultimately, literature, which was his real passion. The path also included eschewing the family diamond business. "I guess I was the first member of my family not to go into my father's business, which was more or less obligatory," he says. "But I thought that since I was in America, I was going to go my own way."

Tytell's interest in the Beat Generation began while in graduate school and he edited an anthology for Harper & Row called *The American Experience: A Radical Reader*. "The book was one of the first attempts to understand the turbulence of that era and its publication caused some notoriety," Tytell says. His interest was further piqued by the torrent of negative reception the Beats received during the 60s. "The establishment critics had positioned the Beats as the new barbarians at the gates," he says. "Kerouac was called the "Latrine Laureate" by *Time*. When his masterpiece, *Visions of Cody*, was posthumously published in 1973, I was asked to review it for *Partisan Review*. I was knocked out by the book; just overwhelmed by the sheer rhapsody of its rhythmic power. So that became a motive for me: to tell what I had discovered to a larger public. That's what any literary or social critic should want to do."

When Tytell was hired by Queens College in the sixties, it was as a specialist on Henry James, the subject of his graduate dissertation. "When I first proposed that I wanted to teach a course on the Beats, they said, 'No way. You teach Henry James.' So I taught the first course on the Beats in America at the New School instead, then at Rutgers, and then Queens finally decided to let me start doing it there. Every time I taught that course it was major enrollment. It made my colleagues who were teaching Victorian literature feel a little inadequate! I'm still teaching the course."

An ad in the Village Voice in 1967 led Tytell and his wife to their apartment on Perry Street. "I thought the West Village was the most beautiful part of Manhattan. I grew up on Riverside Drive where the buildings make you feel claustrophobic so I loved the architecture and the light here. Plus, it had a music scene and a bar scene that you couldn't find anywhere else. That represented a kind of freedom for me. It was the only part of the city I could see myself living in."

"When we moved here it was much more working class in our building," he remembers. "They were all ordinary people working ordinary jobs. One family were even longshoremen. The docks were still active in those days and a lot of people in the neighborhood worked on them. And the neighborhood shops were all Mom and Pop grocery stores. Of course, things have changed drastically since then." He pauses to consider for a moment and then laughs. "But everything changes all the time and smart people go with the flow!"

Summing up a life spent in the West Village, Tytell puts it all in perspective. "I've been delighted and privileged to be here," he says. "Both my wife and I have never wanted to leave. We've lived all over the world, but we're always so happy to come back here. In the final analysis, I think what the Village always represented to me was a sense of possibility, and that's still here."

ACKNOWLEDGMENTS

Heartfelt thanks to George Capsis, the indomitable publisher of *WestView News*, the true voice of the West Village. George cheerfully published each and every one of my West Village Original interviews and never said the paper didn't have room.

Thanks to all the photographers who so kindly gave permission to use their images of those interviewed. Special thanks to Maggie Berkvist, *WestView's* resident photographer, who took many of the portraits in this book and who captured the essence of everyone who posed for her.

Thanks to Ted DuBois, publisher of Bios Books, for convincing me to publish this collection of interviews.

Thanks to my father, Robert, now 98 years old, who always encouraged me to write.

INDEX

Amram, David, p. 96
Benepe, Barry, p. 10
Bensusan, Danny, p. 14
Berger, Keen, p. 34
Berkvist, Maggie, p. 114
Berman, Andrew, p. 36
Block, Frederic, p. 38
Bogen, Nancy, p. 190
Borgatta, Isabel Case, p. 170
Brownmiller, Susan, p. 192
Busch, Charles, p. 136
Cannistraci, Lisa, p. 16
Carlaftes, Peter, p. 138
Chase, Suzy, p. 62
Cole, Rainie, p. 140
Collier, James Lincoln, p. 86
Colt, Marjorie, p. 172
Curreri, Bill, p. 98
Del Tredici, David, p. 100
Dowling, Jack, p. 194
Dunham, Bill, p. 102
Field, Edward, p. 130
Garson, Barbara, p. 142
Gilbert, Elliott, p. 174
Gilman, John, p. 196
Goldsteinn, Bobb, p. 104
Grange, Carmen, p. 40
Greenspan, David, p. 144
Gruber, David, p. 42
Gruen, Bob, p. 116
Hall, Stephen, p. 176
Ham, Larry, p. 106
Hartman, Rose, p. 118
Harvey, Peter, p. 178
Heide, Robert, p. 146
Held, George, p. 132
Hughes, Gordon, p. 148
Jones, Penny, p. 150
Johnson, Page, p. 74
Kramer, Karen, p. 76
Lee, Ralph, p. 44
Leitch, Peter, p. 108
Lerner, Erwin, p. 152
Lisi, Joe, p. 78
Livelli, Vincent, p. 66
Lo, Anita, p. 64
Marsa, Denise, p. 110
Mason, Marshall W., p. 154
McAllister, Joan, p. 46

Meyerowitz, Rick, p. 180
Michael, Keith, p. 48
Mignatti, Victor, p. 80
Morfee, Scott, p. 156
O'Donnell, Bill, p. 18
Paisner, Dina, p. 158
Paley, Ethel, p. 50
Perry, Nicky, p. 20
Phelan, Stephanie, p. 22
Pilikian, Allen, p. 52
Plakke, David, p. 120
Poli, Suzanne, p. 122
Polshek, James Stewart, p. 12
Quinton, Everett, p. 160
Repicci, William, p. 162
Revland, Catherine, p. 198
Riddle, Barbara, p. 200
Romp, Billy, p. 24
Rothenberg, David, p. 54
Rubenfeld, Andrew, p. 202
Rudolph, Nancy, p. 124
Sage, Sybil, p. 82
Schoenfeld, Kika, p. 182
Schwartz, Arthur Z., p. 56
Seymour, Jr., Whitney North, p. 58
Sharp, David Maurice, p. 26
Sheraton, Mimi, p. 88
Staller, Jan, p. 126
Stephen, Edith, p. 68
SuZen, p. 128
Tango, Jenny, p. 184
Three Lives & Company, p. 28
Tomas, Salvador Peter, p. 164
Trillin, Calvin, p. 90
Tytell, John, p. 204
Vaccaro, Mary, p. 186
Van Asselt, David, p. 166
Vetra, Vija, p. 70
Warwick, Arnold S., p. 30
Weber, Nancy, p. 92
Weigle, Richard Eric, p. 84

www.ingramcontent.com/pod-product-compliance
Lightning Source LLC
Chambersburg PA
CBHW042112120526
44592CB00042B/2701